You Are Already Praying

You Are Already PRAYING

Stories of God at Work

Cathy George

Morehouse Publishing

NEW YORK · HARRISBURG · DENVER

Morehouse Publishing, 4775 Linglestown Road,
Harrisburg, PA 17112

Morehouse Publishing, 445 Fifth Avenue,
New York, NY 10016

Morehouse Publishing is an imprint of
Church Publishing Incorporated.

www.churchpublishing.org

Cover design by Laurie Klein Westhafer
Typeset by Denise Hoff

Library of Congress
Cataloging-in-Publication Data

A catalog record of this book is available from the
Library of Congress.

ISBN-13: 978-0-8192-2853-6 (pbk.)
ISBN-13: 978-0-8192-2854-3 (ebook)

Printed in the United States of America

CONTENTS

You are the future,
The red sky before sunrise
Over the fields of time.

You are the cock's crow when night is done,
You are the dew and the bells of matins,
Maiden, stranger, mother, death.

You create yourself in ever-changing shapes
That rise from the stuff of our days–
Unsung, unmourned, undescribed,
Like a forest we never knew.

You are the deep innerness of all things,
The last word that can never be spoken.
To each of us you reveal yourself differently:
To the ship as coastline, to the shore as a ship.

From *The Book of Pilgrimage*
—Rainer Marie Rilke[1]

1   *Rilke's Book of Hours: Love Poems to God,* Anita Barrows and
    Joanna Marie Macy, trans. (New York: Riverhead Trade, 2005), 177.
    Used by permission.

INTRODUCTION

Pray without ceasing.

—1 Thessalonians 5:17

THIS BOOK IS about the prayer that already goes on in our lives. Maybe you commute by bus to three minimum wage jobs to pay the rent and cover your child's tuition. Or perhaps your professional prominence is accompanied by a grueling schedule. Maybe you cook and serve, and go home to do the same, or you run meetings, crunch numbers, draw blood, hire people, fire them, or teach school. Our lives are filled with civic and family commitments, neighborhood meetings, church leadership, social relationships: complete my list with your own responsibilites! Life is full. You are busy working several jobs to cover the cost of a parent's medical care; or you own a restaurant and the hours are endless. Physicians and scientists, carpenters and realtors, you who work in the home caring for a household, children, or elder loved ones: you are already praying.

After high school, my dad worked in a hardware store before being drafted into the Navy. After his tour of duty, he worked as a carpenter, eventually owning a construction company, building and remodeling custom homes. When our pastor was on vacation, my dad was invited to preach. The congregation loved his sermons: he got right to the point and talked in his normal voice, not a "churchy" one, and often used memorable props. Noticing spiritual gifts in those not ordained began as I watched my dad.

In its ancient, monastic form, prayer was what a monk or nun did in chapel—and when they set out from chapel, their prayer continued in the office, study, field, classroom, and kitchen. Working in a laboratory, managing a staff, performing surgery or caring for a child can be part of a life of prayer. Whether washing the dishes, weeding the garden, or chairing a decisive meeting, we can be at prayer.

I know a monk masterful at spiritual guidance who was invited to speak at a conference and asked to fill the "spiritual block." He replied: "I'm really not interested in spirituality; I am interested in life." When a person came to see him filled with bitterness toward God, his life a series of disappointments, the wise monk advised him to ". . . take up Italian cooking, or plant a rose garden. Forget about God, let God find you in the kitchen or in the garden enjoying your life."

My tradition teaches "prayer is responding to God, by thought and by deeds, with or without words" (*Book of Common Prayer*, Catechism, 856). Voices of many spiritual traditions echo this inclusive definition of prayer. A friend, now in her eighties, tells me "prayer is a form of life." An intern in his early twenties says that his "real work is to live in the presence of God, and express that presence in everything I do. Prayer is a mindset, an attitude, dedicating every act, no matter how seemingly trivial it may be to God. And yes, that goes for doing laundry!"

My work brings me close to the lives of people. After working as a prison chaplain, my work shifted to parish life. In rural, city, suburban, and inner-city parishes, the people that I meet inspire my prayer. As a mother, wife, and priest, I know for myself what I hear from my people: the monastic ideal of a life set apart from the world for prayer is not our life. We need another way. We want our faith and our life to connect. People pray about their work as a doctor, teacher, banker, or limousine driver, but don't call it prayer. They pray for their kids, their friends, and their marriages, but don't think of it as prayer. Respect for the natural world and enjoyment of its beauty feels sacred, but we don't think of it as a prayer. When we create or witness art, it touches our spiritual lives, but we struggle for a language that acknowledges artistic expression as prayer. In sport or physical movement we sense God's presence, but how do we pray in our physical body? Putting our faith into action, doing things for others, giving back may be our way of being spiritual, but can actions be prayers?

Your experience of prayer may not be peaceful or quiet or set apart from your daily life. It may be embedded in the actions you take, the compassion you show, or the art you create. Perhaps prayer moves through you in love and respect for the beauty of the natural world. Or gratitude wells up in you while walking a country road or watching a child at play. Maybe you close the office door and ask God for help, or you try praying on the treadmill at the health club before heading home, or while out on a run, but is that prayer? Maybe you talk to God about your day while commuting but you think you should find a better time for prayer. You feel that all these efforts and attempts somehow fall short of truly being prayer.

Our lives often are too noisy, too conflicted, too worldly, too complicated to have the quality of what we imagine as prayer. And yet, our lives are filled with prayer; prayer in actions, preaching by doing, patience in a moment of trial, stopping for a silent moment before speaking, closing the office door before a difficult decision or meeting. In busy, over-extended, challenging lives, prayer takes a variety of forms: an action, a kindness, an attitude, a hard decision, and a creative endeavor.

Even when we are distracted and busy, sacred moments break through: the nudge to go in one direction and not another, an intuition we're given, the awe that overcomes us as we listen to music. God breaks in as a surge of creativity, a supply of patience, a kind word just when we need it.

A lawyer arguing a case in court, a parent comforting a child, or a postal worker greeting the next person in line: each of us has an opportunity, every day, to treat our life and work as a sacred calling, as holy as the work of a priest at the altar.

Rich, poor, and middle income; black, brown, white, gay, and straight; young people, seniors, and many in their middle years struggle to find time for prayer. If only "prayers-on-the-go" counted as real prayer, we say to ourselves. They do.

It all counts. The desire to connect with God, to pray, is a seed planted within us by the Holy Spirit. We don't plant it, God does. We water it. We foster its growth. And when we do, its branches begin to extend into everything we do, all day long, all week long. Our daily lives become a living prayer—our response to the unceasing presence of God within us and around us.

THE TYRANNY OF TIME

I kept hearing something I didn't want to hear: we don't have time. I blamed the people in the pews. I grew frustrated as I offered more of the programs they asked for but didn't attend. People wanted a children's choir but had no time in their children's afternoon schedule for rehearsals. They wanted Christian education but could not attend church for two hours on a Sunday, as it conflicted with sports schedules. People arrived late and hungry to week-night meetings, coming straight from work. Couples brought kids to Sunday school and sat in their car to talk to each other rather than coming to our adult forum, just to find time together. Get a grip, own your time, and take some control over your life, I thought to myself. Frustrated by my attempts to make church a priority in the lives of busy people,

I changed what I was doing. I cancelled the Lenten series I had planned and designed one called, *Take Back Your Time*. We gathered as a community and talked honestly about time.

People came. Every chair in the large fellowship hall was filled. People talked about the binds they were in. How trapped and guilty they felt. Travel schedules demanded so much time away from family, while others at work waited in line for a chance at their job. Competing demands left them in turmoil over how they spent their time, usually feeling guilty about what they could not find time to do. "This is no way to live, but what can I do, where do I turn?" I wasn't content to have church be one more demand on the calendar; it needed to give the life it promises. Inside the church, we focused on the struggles we faced outside the church. We didn't have perfect answers, but openly addressing the problem and sharing it helped. We realized what good company we were in. Our community grew closer to one another by sharing a burden many were bearing alone.

We discussed Abraham Heschel's fantastic (and thin!) book *Sabbath* and came up with ways to encourage each other to manage our time focused on our values. We came to the conclusion that we, as a church, needed to change the way we did things. We changed our parish meeting style and schedule, added a "Come as You Are" Sunday evening service, and began to focus on our daily lives as places of prayer. We acknowledged that prayer on a walk or during the commute was, indeed, prayer—that our interactions with nature and art, with other people, our actions at work and home could all be ways of praying, places for us to invite God into our life that held the potential to bring us closer to God. This book is designed to offer you those same affirmations. Your life—just as it is—is filled with "the deep innerness of all things." You are already praying.

1

PRAYER IN WORK

WHATEVER OUR LIFE'S work, opportunities exist for us to be instruments of grace in the lives of those we live and work with. Pushing my cart full of groceries towards the exit door, I stop to show my receipt to the man at the threshold. Each time I have seen him I have noticed a tiny picture of Jesus with a flaming heart at the corner of his name badge. He reviews my receipt, eyeing the items in my cart, and as he hands it back to me I point to Jesus on his badge and smile. He says: "He is the best friend you can have. I take him to work!"

> *Work done in gratitude,*
> *Kindly, and well, is prayer.*
>
> —Wendell Berry[1]

Maude is a patient services manager in the food services department of a large urban hospital. A day does not go by without an opportunity to put her prayer into action in her work. When the hospital

---

1 From "LXXXIII," *A Timbered Choir: The Sabbath Poems 1979–1997* (Berkeley: Counterpoint Press, 1999), 141.

conducted contract reviews for five departments, food service, Maude's department, was the only one that kept its contract. Maude attributes this to putting her prayer to action. "I am a child of God and I realized I cannot let anything happen to the job security of those who work for me." She met day after day with her supervisors, and those who worked for her, coming up with compromises and solutions to present to the review board. "Right there in the middle of our meeting, I said: God is not going to shut one door and not open another. They seemed to listen to me!" Maude said with a smile.

As new contracts were signed across the hospital's departments, Maude watched people she worked with for years lose their jobs, with nothing to show for their years of work. "I think the way we treat each other at work matters. I am kind to everyone I work with, not just when I feel like it, or when I like someone, or when they can do something good for me. No, because God is watching and God is with me. You know, it blesses me right back. God's blessed me with this job, and with two kids and two grandkids. I have to bless others for all that is given to me." And she does.

Maude was raised in the Caribbean; her mother, father, and 11 brothers and sisters grew up in the Anglican Church. "You didn't go to church if you felt like it, you went to church, every single Sunday, no matter what. How you treated people, how you behaved, how you spoke, it all mattered. In fact my mother would give us the evil eye at church if we were not in her good graces because we did something wrong that week. When it came time for communion, she'd say, 'Oh no you don't' and hold you back in the pew if you had done something wrong." Maude laughed just picturing her mother's arm going out in front of her brothers and sisters as they were told to sit back down in the pew. "We were taught that life is about loving and serving God, all the time, in all you do. I cannot go away from that teaching," Maude says. "If I try to hold back and not bring my faith in God to work every day, something tells me, 'Maude, you've left something behind, go get it.'"

I met Maude when I came to her parish in the inner city. She was an usher and a member of the vestry. Once we became acquainted, the second year of my term in her parish, she invited me to an awards ceremony at the hospital where she worked. Along with two doctors from her hospital, Maude was there to receive the M. L. King Jr. service award at a ceremony in the hospital auditorium. She stood at the podium, 5 feet 11 inches tall in a beautiful cranberry dress with a corsage pinned at the neckline. Before she was given the award, her supervisor told the story of her dedication to the patients she served.

A young female patient suffering with cancer came to Maude's attention on floor rounds. She refused to eat and was losing weight. Maude knew the young woman was from the islands and talked to her about foods from home: curried goat and stewed chicken, fried fish, rice, black-eyed peas, and beef pies. Day after day Maude went to the kitchen and found food she knew the young woman would eat and had it sent up to her. The young woman died, and Maude attended her funeral to extend her sympathy to the young woman's family. When she met the woman's father, he told her he was looking for a "lady from the islands" his daughter spoke about on the telephone from the hospital. "She worked in food services and was always there for my daughter. I want to thank her."

I knew why Maude invited me to the awards ceremony that day. As her priest, I represented her faith community. She wanted the people she worked with to know that the source of this award, the impetus behind the kind of employee she was, came from her faith in God, from her decision to bring her prayer to work with her. I sat in the audience in the hospital auditorium feeling proud of Maude. Maude was invited forward to receive her award. She moved to the podium, thanked people from the hospital staff, and congratulated the two physicians who were her fellow recipients. Then she did something I was unprepared for: she introduced me and asked me to come forward and speak.

I was honored to be there; those words came easily. I thanked Maude and the two doctors being honored for the inspiration their work was to me. One further comment came to my mind and I shared it before sitting down. Heads all across the audience nodded "yes" as I spoke. "This is where God goes to work, here in this hospital, through your hands, and your skills, your patience and determination and compassion. When God's love is expressed in the world as we have heard it is today in the lives of the three people you have honored, representing the work of so many others, then we know God is alive. How we choose to do the work we do is how we pray back our thanks to God for all we have been given."

Maude and I walked out together into the hospital corridor, where she introduced me to the person who nominated her for the award. "I was a young mother when I met Maude," she said. "I worked as a dietician and handed Maude my resignation the day my day care fell through. She told me to come to her office and 'sit down.' She called one place after another until she found day care for my daughter close enough to the hospital for me to keep my job." Maude smiled and said "and she got one promotion after another and now she supervises the nutrition department." Nodding her head yes, the young woman exclaimed with a wide smile on her face, "And now I am your boss!"

David is a pediatric neurologist whose prayer accompanies him to work:

I majored in French literature in college and went to France to study. By what I then called chance, I met a French neurologist who was looking for an American to check the accuracy of translation of a standard clinical language test from English into French, to make certain the colloquial elements had been done justice. I did the work. Afterwards, he offered to let me come to his office as he field-tested the new instrument. I was thoroughly hooked. I fell on the study of the brain with passion, delight, devotion. It gave what had felt like a rudderless course direction and purpose. I changed my entire track, I repented in the oldest sense of the word and came back to the U.S. intending to become not only a physician, but more specifically a neurologist.

This trajectory certainly distinguished me from many of my medical school peers in those days, particularly the absence of any significant laboratory science background. Science drawing a person to the medical field is a well-worn path; following a clinical passion was a bit less usual. I arrived to become a neurologist because I had somehow fallen in love with the whole clinical spectrum of neurology. Like most love affairs, it would be difficult to explain to someone who was not as infatuated as I was: to explain the object of my affection, the why and the how and the when.

I eventually found myself taking an elective hardly anyone else ever signed on for: outpatient neurology clinics. My favorite part of the

*month was seeing patients with the man who
would shortly thereafter become my mentor—
the training director of the residency and
education programs, a quiet, reserved, cryptic
man given to understated observations, the
poetry of William Carlos Williams, the history of neurology, and a sardonic view of the
tempests that often stirred the medical school
teapot.*

*I looked at the calendar one evening and
saw that a patient had been assigned the
usual hour for a new visit, and the subse-
quent hour crossed out, closed and unavail-
able. I wondered what that meant. I asked,
and he just grunted, "Well, you'll see."*

*In any event, the patient, drooling slightly,
but dressed quite elegantly, arrived with her
husband. An older woman, her clothing and
demeanor were that of a more gracious era
than we inhabited. Her husband was dapper,
solicitous, clearly worried. It started when
she experienced trouble speaking, slurring her
words (at first, her husband admitted with a
blush, he thought she'd been "tippling at lun-
cheon"). Then she began to complain that she
had trouble chewing and swallowing certain
foods. At night, she began to snore. The first
time she choked over supper her husband
realized that her condition was something
that needed medical attention. He took her to*

their internist, who said little, save that they needed to see a neurologist. Soon.

The internist had called my mentor, who cleared his evening clinic for this appointment. He took the history in a way that was gentle but probing. He reassured the woman he had no wish to embarrass her, but needed to know certain things. Ever so quietly, he asked question after question, to which she usually answered something in the affirmative, her eyes manifesting relief that someone seemed to understand what had been happening to her. Her husband was showing an increasing sense of foreboding [that] her symptoms seemed to be leading somewhere.

My mentor then examined her with the quiet-and-gentle-but-determined manner his questions employed. I was in awe—his hands, his reflex hammer, his tuning fork—all seemed instruments of some graceful music I could only barely hear.

After a time, he sat down. "Well," he said, "we need to talk. The roots of the nerves that care for the muscles of your face and throat and neck, the nerves that arise from what we call the brainstem, where the brain and spinal cord meet, are dying. As a result, the muscles in those places no longer follow your will. This is a problem that will progress, inevitably and unrelentingly, and I am afraid I can offer nothing to stop it.

"It will make it difficult, and then impossible, to swallow, or smile, or talk, and eventually to breathe. You have a disease called amyotrophic lateral sclerosis, sometimes called Lou Gehrig's disease. You have a form we call bulbar ALS, because it involves the brainstem. It is untreatable, and progressive."

We sat in silence for a while. She began to whimper, then sniffle, then cry, then let out a great keening wail that filled the room. It felt like her cry would fill the entire floor and then the building and then the whole hospital campus. Her husband threw his arms around her and began to sob.

My mentor sat there, watching them both, with sad and clear eyes. He said nothing. After a time, their crying slowed down, and they both looked at him.

"Is that it?" the husband asked. "Is there nothing else? Is there nothing we can do? Is there nothing to be done?"

"I can do nothing, I'm afraid," said my mentor. "We cannot treat this disease. But I will never leave you. I will never abandon you. We will all see this through to the end."

They sat for a while, and then asked what they should do next. "This is a lot to take in. Perhaps we should see each other next week, if that's all right with you," said my mentor. They smiled wanly, and said, "Oh yes, please."

"Good," he said. "The secretary will make some time for you next week."

They walked out.

He sat there, very quietly, for what seemed like a very long time. He then looked at me. "This is what we do," he said. "This is really what our discipline is about. Death, and as much truth and kindness as you can possibly bring up in the face of death. You need to know that, if you want to spend your life doing this."

And so I began to learn that hard lesson, the first of many along the path I have followed. But I also learned something about prayer, presence, gift, and gratitude. The first prayer I ever experienced at work was just this. Clear-eyed, honest, hard-won compassion, and a willingness to stand by someone in the valley of the shadow of death.

Jesus worked. His father Joseph worked, with a plane and a lathe and a pencil behind his ear. Mary had duties in the temple and household, working to wash and mend clothes, preparing food, caring for neighbors and friends in need. How did they, and countless others who have gone before us, work and pray?

In the collection of essays, *Professions of Faith: Living and Working as a Catholic*, Lucie Fjeldstad writes about the challenge of mentoring and guiding her company. Jesus was her role model, but instead of bringing religious quotes, church documents, or the sacraments into the business, she introduced Christian values and ethics. "Valuing people and operating with integrity, bringing a heart, character, and conscience" into their business model is what she sought to do. Those values became more important than money, and consequently the money became a by-product of a business that was respected and respected others. At the close of her essay, she concludes that she discovered she was "far more religious than I have given myself credit for." Her discovery is one we can all make.[2]

Once Philip cultivated a pathway and opened his heart, God was never far away. He feels God's presence most acutely in his work. "No matter what my state of mind on any given day, God and I, without words, gather together to prepare a sacred space for all who enter. Like an old married couple, for 30 years we have been cooperating like this together. God begins some of my thoughts, and I finish some of God's." Philip's prayer at work is not in the form of words, his intention is to embody prayer in his actions. "My life's work is my ministry as a full-time clinical psychologist and therapist, a full-time partner and family caregiver," Philip tells me. "My work for the church is not more ministry, or more God directed than my work during the week as a

2   Lucie Fjeldstad, "Building on a Firm Foundation: On Being a
    Catholic Business Person," in *Professions of Faith: Living and
    Working as a Catholic,* James Martin and Jeremy Langford, eds.
    (Lanham, MD: Rowman and Littlefield, 2002), 17–25.

therapist, or my devotion to my partner and family. They are all my life's work, and I need prayer to see me through each of them." Early in what Philip calls his spiritual evolution, "God broke into my awareness like a favorite Aunt who arrives unexpectedly on your doorstep."

Jim is a Landscape Architect.

My favorite image of how prayer intersects with work is from the film "Chariots of Fire." Olympic champion and committed Christian Eric Liddell talks about his experience when running; "I believe God made me for a purpose, but he also made me fast. And when I run, I feel His pleasure." Feeling God's pleasure and our own, simultaneously, captures for me the experience of prayer and its integration into what I do most of my days. It is about finding and utilizing our gifts. Eric's gift is running. When he runs he loses himself and is filled with joy. I have experienced this oneness, flow, and effortlessness in my work. It's not an everyday occurrence.

As I contemplate work as prayer, it raises questions about who I am and what I do. It unsettles me. It does not give me peace or comfort about my living reality. Perhaps if I were a teacher, minister, or social worker this would all be easier! And, I imagine, it would be even more difficult if I worked on Wall Street—or for a weapons manufacturer.

There are three aspects of my work as prayer: WHAT I do, HOW I do it, and my RELATIONSHIPS with the people with whom I work.

WHAT I do. I ask myself: is my business, the goods and services that I provide, within the scope of God's will or purposes? This can be a tough one. I have many opportunities to design landscapes or participate in land development projects that may be profitable and prestigious but that violate many of my faith-inspired, ethical, and environmental convictions. What's good for business, good for the land, and good for people aren't always the same things. So I have lost projects, struggled with building my firm, and had difficulties keeping employees while trying to hang on to the values that are important to me. At times I get cynical. I cave in to the norm, to business as usual. I tell myself: the customer is always right (which they rarely are). To be successful, I need to give people what they want and exceed their expectations, doing the work faster, and cheaper. This is not work as prayer.

If I follow the "business as usual" mode

and look outwards, following the trends of other companies, making all decisions based on economic practicalities, I lose the divine connection to my work. I have had to reinvent my business a couple times and adjust it again and again so that what I do is a reflection of who I am and the gifts God has given me.

In the mid-1980s the economy was good. I was a Yuppie with 13 employees, an office of my own, a beautiful young family, and everything was going great! Inside, however, I was stressed and miserable. I had frequent migraines. I had an outwardly successful business that was not a reflection of myself and did not utilize my gifts in design and drawing. My commitment to creating natural and sustainable landscapes was rarely manifest and was actually undermined by serving customers who didn't care about the environment at all. To work with a sense of my own integrity and follow God's call was more difficult. It was an obscure choice and it was easier to follow the conventional path in my industry. I have struggled with this dilemma for over thirty years. And I have done both. I have taken projects that simply put "bread on the table," and I have been fortunate enough to do some inspired work that is leading-edge and pushes the envelope of how people can live more sustainably on the land. The meaningful work was easy and flowed out of me—like prayer. And it made a difference and it will be remembered. As for my other, more typical work, which I regret to say consumed most of my days, energy and worry—in the long run, it didn't matter and will soon fade away.

Prayer also affects HOW I work. Gratitude is the most helpful for me. Starting each day with a prayer of thanks and appreciation for health, family, and meaningful work makes a difference. Being grateful for simply having work, for my clients and for my employees. Gratitude solves all sorts of problems! I become more purposeful and energetic and show appreciation to those I work with. When I forget, get stressed and overloaded, coming back to thankfulness changes my mood and outlook. Late in the summer I often take time to photograph landscape projects that have matured, ones I designed and built a few years back. It's always exciting and ener-gizing for me to see my work and to see how it has grown and developed over the years. There are always some surprises, things I hadn't planned on. The experience of docu-menting what I have done over time is always instructive and reinvigorates me as to my call and my purpose.

When I feel this sense of purpose, working long hours, being disciplined and keeping a positive attitude seem to take care of themselves.

When I lose that prayerful connection, I get tired and resentful and lose creativity. There are times when I get into drawing or arranging the elements in a landscape composition and I lose track of time, like the runner in Chariots of Fire. That might be an indicator of when my work is indeed prayer. Doing what we love with no sense of time (or money) seems to be the ideal state. Needless to say, I don't spend my whole workweek like this.

For me, God is a dynamic, living force, and my work needs to be too. I experiment with new plants and materials, soils, and stones. There are always new ideas about people and their relationship to their land that bring new opportunities for expression and exploration. Trends towards more sustainable design, native plants, locally grown vegetables, and recycled materials all provide new opportunities to discover something new—and divine— in my work.

When my work is prayer, the RELATIONSHIPS I have at work are much better. As Bob Dylan says, "You've got to serve somebody," and an attitude of service is always great for customer satisfaction! It also gives me a sense of purpose and meaning to have served others and done my best. Whether or not service is always a prayer, I am not sure, but it feels like it is. An attitude of service takes me and my ego needs out of the equation and allows for better, more inspired things to happen.

When confronted by difficult clients and customer service issues I often ask for inspiration or seek God's solutions, ones I cannot see. This "letting go" helps reduce tension and worry and often makes room for creative, new solutions. I can recall instances when I have presented a design concept to a client and they didn't like it. My ego, expertise, and income are very much on the line. Letting go rather than arguing or compromising my work is usually the most helpful path. Sometimes it comes back as a wise step and other times, it's all a wash. But "giving it up" alleviates the feeling that "it's all about me."

Running a small business, I am my own human resource department. I need help with it. My training is technical and in the arts. My weakness is people skills and communication. Having to deal with salaries, benefits, paid time off, hiring, and termination is the most difficult part of having my own business. I feel overwhelmed and incompetent. I prefer to avoid this stuff. Sometimes I seek out a higher power—a different perspective— as I am forced to address these issues with employees. I recall being pressured and made to feel guilty by a designer-salesperson who asked for a lucrative compensation package when his performance didn't come close to deserving it. This was difficult to communicate to him. We reviewed the issues and numbers several times over several months and when I finally had to let him go, he still showed up at work the next Monday! In front of other employees I had to talk it over again and clarify what he would not accept. These kind of difficult situations require a mix of compassion, firmness, and spiritual integration that I can only hope for. I lifted this person and my responsibilities in prayer many times during that year. Years have passed, and this young man has moved on and we are once again on good terms.

Recently, I had a young employee who was constantly running out of money. He talked me into advancing money on his pay several times and always asked when the paychecks could be picked up. Then he started filling up his car with gas on the company account without permission. We had to talk. I recall praying for help and guidance as to what to do. I could have (perhaps should have) fired him right then. However, it helped to talk to him. I expressed my observations and concerns, and we worked out a plan for reimbursement. I think it was a growth opportunity for both of us—he heard some things about right and wrong but was still accepted and I got a chance to better understand his situation and learn to be firm and patient. I felt that I had divine help navigating through this situation. I didn't let it slide (my most favored path, leading to resentment) and I wasn't reactive or angry. I experienced my work as prayer.

Sharyn works as an administrator at a community college. "Most of my prayer is in the car. I have a long commute, so I find myself praying when I start out by giving God thanks for the beauty of the day. I give thanks for my work and family, and when I arrive at work, I try to begin with a prayer, short and to the point, asking God to help me listen and not be judgmental."

Sharyn never thought that higher education administration would be a place to practice her faith. "Some people say that we should not talk about politics and religion at work, but I am amazed how many people at work share their faith with me; Christians, Jews, and fellow Episcopalians. Someone will email me or come to my office to tell me about something that is going on that they know I will be interested in. It adds an important dimension to work to share my spiritual life with others in the workplace. I was explaining to a Jew and Muslim what Lent is, and it resulted in talking about things that bring meaning to our workday. Once I was discussing life's difficulties and discovered that the person I spoke with used the same simple words to guide him as I do: "Love your neighbor as yourself." Simple but hard to put into practice.

*Dying people have the power to heal
the rest of us in unusual ways.*

—Dr. Rachel Naomi Remen[3]

Jeanie is a hospice nurse:

*It was my first solo visit. Nervous hardly
begins to describe my feeling as I pulled up
to the address. The house was dark and
cluttered. "He's upstairs," the elderly woman
whispered. The strong and distinctively bad
odor hit me as I walked up the narrow,
creaky stairs. Tentatively, I walked into the
room and saw this old, thin, and dying man,
lying in his own mess . . . stool everywhere—
covering his body, on his hands and in his
fingernails, on the sheets and blankets. Even
the bar of soap and the water faucets had
brown on them.*

*I was overwhelmed, revolted, and dis-
gusted. God's grace found a way to break
through my reactions. "Help me, please. Help
me through this and help me to see him
in his truth, a child of God." From beyond
my mind, I was filled with actual love as I*

---

3   In *Kitchen Table Wisdom* (New York: Riverhead Trade Publishers,
1997), 255.

cleaned him and changed sheets and tried to make him comfortable. It was shocking to me. It was not me. I was totally grossed out and yet God filled me with love and concern and compassion. I will never forget it. I could not have done it without God. Yes, I would have cleaned him and done my job. But that I felt compassion and love—that was of God.

Gloria was dying with a gaping, smelly, untreatable wound on her neck, where the cancer had eaten through. And Gloria was a blessing to me and to pretty much anyone who interacted with her. In "end-of-life" care, we talk a lot about healing—not physical healing . . . healing between family members, spouses, parents and children; between the dying person and their own God; healing of the individual in relationship to themselves. Many of us reach death's door without ever loving and befriending ourselves. Gloria was in extreme pain and was using all of her energy to deal with it. When hospice first came in, she sat in her wheelchair, head hung, no eye contact, no conversing. She wasn't my patient, but a short time after she started hospice, I was out to see her again, to change the dressing on her neck wound. I cannot describe the beautiful, sparkly eyed, radiantly smiling woman that welcomed me into her home. With her pain well controlled, her healing spirit filled the room. Everyone who came into contact with her was blessed, including me.

I rely on God constantly in my work. There are plenty of times when I don't want to be working, when I'm concerned with my own life or I'm too busy or troubled. I need to pray before I enter a home. I ask God to help me be there, to be present for this individual and family. Help me to do no harm and please use me to be a source of comfort. When I can be present with someone, all there, then I feel we are in the presence of God. My work informs my faith and my life by reminding me that we are all dying and that the present moment is all we have.

Martha is a professor of ethics. The stories of the biblical Martha inspire her work and prayer.

The First Story of Martha

Now as they went on their way, he entered a certain village, where a woman named Martha welcomed him into her home. She had a sister named Mary, who sat at the Lord's feet and listened to what he was saying.

*But Martha was distracted by her
many tasks; so she came to him and
asked, "Lord, do you not care that my
sister has left me to do all the work
by myself? Tell her then to help me."
But the Lord answered her, "Martha,
Martha, you are worried and distracted by many things; there is need
of only one thing. Mary has chosen the
better part, which will not be taken
away from her." (Luke 10:38–42)*

The Second Story of Martha

*When Martha heard that Jesus
was coming, she went out and met
him, while Mary stayed at home.
Martha said to Jesus, "Lord, if you
had been here, my brother would
not have died. But even now I know
that God will give you whatever you
ask of him." Jesus said to her, "Your
brother will rise again." Martha said
to him, "I know that he will rise
again in the resurrection on the last
day." Jesus said to her, "I am the
resurrection and the life. Those who
believe in me, even though they die,
will live, and everyone who lives and
believes in me will never die. Do you
believe this?" She said to him, "Yes,*

Lord. I believe that you are the Messiah, the Son of God, the one coming into the world." (John 11:20–27)

These two stories of my biblical namesake bookend a life. Together they speak a truth that neither one quite captures on its own. Over the course of almost six decades, they have worked like alchemy in the personal and professional dimensions of my life.

Luke's portrait of the worried, burdened Martha buttresses the beginning. Even as a child, I was a worker, aiming for excellence. I remember walking home from Rodger's Forge Elementary School, a distance of about ten blocks in a development built along the lines of Baltimore's fabled brick row houses. Every time my right foot hit the pavement, I would whisper "excellence." It put a stride in my gait that is still there.

How does such ferocity come to a grade-school girl? It wasn't parental pressure, but medical fluke. Early photos showed a slight list to one of her eyes. This was quickly diagnosed as amblyopia, but the explanation given to the child was "lazy" eye syndrome, or even occasionally, "a bad eye." Like the first story of Martha from Luke, she caught the rebuke. "Lazy" was something she wanted no part of. Moreover, if any part of her was to be "bad," it would be on her own terms.

Surgery was recommended, and the five year old had an operation to "correct" her vision. General anesthesia blocked pain, but even a drugged patient watches eye surgery. For years, the child had nightmares of people in masks, armed with sharp instruments and hovering over her face.

For the doctors at Johns Hopkins, surgery was a simple matter of relaxing the muscles in the "good" eye, a procedure medically preferable to tightening the muscles in the "bad" one. For the child, though, surgery bore all the spiritual freight of exorcism. It promised to rid her forever of sloth, not to mention evil. In fact, the immediate result gave her two "bad" eyes. When the bandages came off, she couldn't see much of anything.

Years of patches and eye exercises followed, as the child worked to train her eyes to work together. Her father spent hours playing catch with her, throw by throw rebuilding eye-hand coordination. He took her downtown to one of the old historic buildings around Mount Vernon Place, where the eye specialist, Miss Smith, peered, poked, and put in drops.

The worst part of each visit, though, was the invariant question: "How many fingers am I holding up?" The child deduced that with one hand in the air, thumb and three fingers folded down, Miss Smith held up only one finger. Yet, she always saw two. No amount of effort on her part could produce one finger.

"How many fingers am I holding up?" Should the child tell the truth of her eyes? Or the truth of the fingers? Each answer would be partly a lie. But each answer would also be partly the truth. In a manner both brutal and gracious, the child learned that truths can be multiple. That insight exiled her forever from the black-and-white moral landscape of childhood. Real life happened in a great grey area. Nothing and no one was completely innocent. But nothing and no one was completely guilty.

Is it any wonder that I went into ethics? Eye exercises were great training for a field that searches for clarity and uncovers only ambiguity: multiple truths. About this time, I stumbled upon an optometrist who captured the truths of both life and my eyes. I was in the middle of an explanation, which was really an apology, for my "poor" vision, and he said: "What do you mean? You see things, don't you? This is simply the way you do it: you triangulate, looking first out of one eye, then the other, to behold the object in between." He offered a medical judgment; I took it as blessing. He gave me a metaphor for work, for prayer, and for work as prayer.

An optometrist's blessing offered me a different perspective on my work.

More obliquely, an optometrist's blessing offered me a different perspective on prayer. Most prayers tend toward bossiness, ordering God to do one thing or another: "Heal us . . . Give us . . . Grant us . . . ." Prayer offers great practice in the grammatical case that handles command. A linguist in Mary Doria Russell's evocative novel, The Sparrow, observes that the best way to learn the imperative in another language is to study its lullabies. Prayer works even better. Eloquent or not, it trades in demands.

But prayer isn't only about demand. Its native language is blessing. About the same time I received the optometrist's blessing, a wise woman offered similar wisdom. While her husband taught religion at my college, she lived it. We talked of a mutual friend, another enormously gifted professor who had struggled with addiction. She confided: "I hardly know what to wish for him. I simply ask that God 'Behold and bless. Behold and bless. Behold and bless.'" She used the language of the optometrist, which I considered more than mere coincidence. At the time, it seemed a revelation that prayer could be—and be prayer—without demanding an outcome. It seemed a revelation that prayer could simply be asking God to behold someone—and bless.

Against the backdrop of my struggle with vision, the insight came as consolation. It pushed me beyond the theologian's question: "How shall we consider God?" and into the contemplative's: "How does God consider us?" In that moment I knew: God simply beholds us—and blesses.

"Behold and bless": the words reframed prayer. With a certainty I'd never had in Miss Smith's office, I discovered a world according to God. God's vision reaches beyond "good" and "bad," beyond "lazy" and "industrious," beyond Mary and Martha alike, even beyond the great simuls of my native Lutheranism, simul justus et peccator, "both saint and sinner." God sees each of us as God saw Jesus: "This is my Son, the Beloved; with you I am well pleased" (Mark 1:11, paraphrased). The divine gaze is unitary and pure: there's no need to triangulate. We are simply beheld— and blessed. I hold onto that prayer like a dog with a bone.

"Behold and bless": the blessing allows me to understand my work as prayer. It offers fresh perspective, not only on myself, but on my colleagues and my students. Although I teach theology, I work with people. It's worth adopting a God's-eye view.

On one hand, the workplace demands out-comes. It calibrates success or failure in terms of achieving them. This prayer leaves the "outcomes" line deliberately blank: God gets to decide.

On the other hand, though, freed from out-comes, everything comes as blessing. For the workplace always throws curveballs. A good colleague can swing at whatever comes across the plate—and still make it to first. Plan A goes awry; the funding for Plan B didn't come through. Can we get behind Plan Q? Yes—200%! Rather than lamenting what we didn't get, we celebrate what comes: blessings abound, even and especially in the workplace.

The crazy thing about blessing is that it leaks. I bless my colleague; he blesses me; our common work blesses our other colleagues and the work of the institution as a whole. Call it a "can-do attitude" or the spirit of "what-the-hellness," if you will. I call it blessing. I just wonder why it took me so long to get a glimpse of this God's-eye view.

Maybe my biblical namesake showed me where to look. The second story of Martha from the Gospel of John serves as the other bookend. In so many ways, this Martha is nothing like the first. Hearing that Jesus is coming, she leaves the house to greet him, moving outside the space reserved for women to enter the space open only to men. Instead of being rebuked for her industry, she rebukes Jesus, challenging him for not being there: "If you had been here, my brother would not have died." That's one perspective. But then she immediately supplies the other: "But even now I know that God will give you whatever you ask of him." Finally, she triangulates and beholds the man in front of her: "I believe that you are the Messiah, the Son of God, the one coming into the world." Her confession stands right up there with Peter's confession at Caesarea Philippi (Mark 8:29; Matthew 16:18). She beholds Jesus—and blesses him.

These two stories of Martha bookend a life; this prayer frames it. On my best days, I get a glimpse of the world according to God. On the lesser days, I know that it's there.

2

PRAYER IN ACTION

Only in our doing can we grasp you.
Only with our hands can we illumine you.
The mind is but a visitor:
It thinks us out of our world.

Each mind fabricates itself.
We sense its limits, for we have made them.
And just when we could flee them, you come
and make of yourself an offering.

I don't want to think a place for you.
Speak to me from everywhere.
Your Gospel can be comprehended
without looking for its source.

When I go toward you
It is with my whole life.

> —From *The Book of a Monastic Life,*
> by Rainer Maria Rilke[1]

---

1   *Rilke's Book of Hours,* 84. Used by permission.

I ATTENDED St. Philip's Church in Harlem on the occasion of the fifth annual celebration of the life of Thurgood Marshall, a former member of the parish. The Supreme Court Justice was honored in an address given by a member of the New York Supreme Court. Her black robe, pleated in front, fell to mid-calf, and the tips of her black shoes were shiny patent leather. She was serious and thorough as she honored the life of someone who prayed in word and deed, someone who took his faith to work.

Thurgood Marshall Academy sat a block away from St. Philip's. Along with libraries, airports, schools, auditoriums, scholarships, and statues across the country similarly named, it is dedicated to the work of a lawyer and judge whose prayers went to work with him in legal studies, policies, and advocacy for those without a voice or power. The achievements in Justice Marshall's life; the actions he took empowering the constitution and laws of his country to work for justice for African Americans and all the disenfranchised, reveals the sacred calling of his faith. His prayer came to fruition in action. His work glorified God as he sought strength to accomplish prayer as action in the world.

Two friends invited us to brunch at a popular local spot in Harlem following the service. We filled our plates with collard greens and ribs, fried chicken, macaroni and cheese, cornbread, green salad, rice and beans. As we feasted in celebration of Thurgood Marshall, we talked about prayer and work. "It is possible," my friend, now a retired nurse, said, his glass of orange juice in hand, "to pray without ceasing. You just have to practice praying no matter what you are doing." He and his partner of 26 years, a psychotherapist, met while consulting on the care of a patient. They noticed from their first professional encounter that the other brought a sense of concern to their mutual work that felt sacred. "We say God is everywhere, and in everything, but it takes practice, it takes paying attention to what you are doing. I have learned to seek God's help and guiding hand as I go about doing *it*, whatever *it* is. It is possible to pray while you work. You have to see prayer as the actions you take. Prayer brings me a great deal of peace when it is chaotic at work. And praying gives me purpose in my work. I am not just doing it for the paycheck, or even for the person I am caring for. I am doing my work for God."

"Pray without ceasing," the Bible tells us. The practice is done by a nurse and psychotherapist who seek the same seamless transition between work and prayer, from Sunday liturgy to the Monday office and hospital that a monastic seeks as they move from the chapel to work in their industry.

Praying in one's actions, outside the walls of church or temple, is a practice like any other. The more we do it, the more we try it, the more we try again without judgment, without evaluating if it was done right or looking for a result from our effort—the more it becomes part of our life. We learn to pray, no matter what. In any mood, or place, or activity. Prayer in action is taking what we are doing, offering it, and forming a habit in our doing and praying that allows the practice of prayer to become a form of life.

The rituals we practice in church are meant to sustain us outside of church. Catholic writer Andre Dubus shares his decidedly sacramental view of life, seeing the sacred nature of ordinary actions and events:

> *A Sacrament is physical and within it is God's love; as a sandwich is physical and nutritious and pleasurable, and within it is love, if someone makes it for you and gives it to you with love; even harried or tired or impatient love, but with love's direction and concern, love's again and again wavering and distorted focus on goodness; then God's love too is in the sandwich.*[2]

---

2   *Broken Vessels: Essays by Andre Dubus* (Boston: David R. Godine, 1992). Used by permission.

Dubus was hit by traffic while stopping to help someone on the highway. He lost his leg and, many surgeries later, was confined to a wheelchair. The ordinary work of parenting—making a sandwich for his daughters when they came home from school—became extraordinary. Each act, now slow and strenuous, spinning his wheelchair to the refrigerator for the mayonnaise and meat, back to the counter for the bread, opening a drawer for a knife to spread mustard, took on the character of a sacrament: an outward sign of the inward love he felt for them. Sandwich making becomes prayer. He writes:

> *I am beginning my ninth year as a cripple, and have learned to move slowly, with concentration, with precision, with peace. Forgetting plastic bags in the first set of drawers and having to turn the chair around to get them is nothing. The memory of having legs that held me upright at this counter and the image of simply turning from the counter and stepping to the drawer are the demons I must keep at bay, or I will rage and grieve because of space, and time, and this wheeled thing that has replaced my legs. So I must try to know the spiritual essence of what I am doing. On Tuesdays when I make lunches for my girls, I focus on this: the sandwiches are sacraments. Not the miracle of transubstantiation, but certainly parallel with it, moving in the same*

direction. If I could give my children my body to eat, again and again without losing it, my body like the loaves and fishes going endlessly in to mouths and stomachs, I would do it. And each moment is a sacrament, this holding of plastic bags, of knives, or bread, of cutting board, this pushing of the chair, this spreading of mustard on bread, this trimming of liverwurst, of ham. All sacraments, as putting the lunches into a zippered book bag and going down my six ramps to my car is. I drive on the highway, to the girls' town, to their school, and this is not simply a transition; it is my love moving by car from a place where my girls are not to a place where they are; even if I do not feel or acknowledge it, this is a sacrament. If I remember it, then I feel it too. Feeling it does not always mean that I am a happy man driving in traffic; it simply means that I know what I am doing in the presence of God.[3]

Stationed at Whidbey Island while serving as a Marine captain, Dubus is called to his father's bedside:

The night flight from Seattle was more than a movement in air from my wife and four young children to my dying father, every moment of it, even as I slept, was a

---

3   *Ibid.*

*sacrament I gave my father; and they were
sacraments he gave me, his siring, and his
love drawing me to him through the night;
and sacraments between my mother and two
sisters and me . . . God's mystery we often
do not clearly see . . . Sacraments came
from those who flew the plane and worked
aboard it and maintained it and controlled
its comings and goings; and from the major
who gave me emergency leave and the gun-
nery sergeant who did my work while I was
gone.*[4]

Prayer in actions may be simple, but not easy.
We discover a connection with God in ordinary
actions we take, and in things we already do and
have never thought of as prayer.

A doctor misses a class he wants to take on
prayer because he devotes one night a week to mentoring and tutoring a promising medical student
from a foreign country working to integrate his education into a new world, but he would never consider
this a prayer. A teacher misses a spiritual direction
group to visit a classmate in the hospital, never con-
sidering her decision, her action to be prayer.

Matt is in his early twenties and works as an
intern: "My job is to help with the day-to-day admin-
istrative functions in a church, accompany the priest
on home visits, help with children's programming,

---

4   *Ibid.*

occasionally give a sermon, and try to facilitate fellowship with the Ugandan Church which shares our building." He goes on to describe what for him is his more vital work: "That's the brief job description, but my work is so much more than that. To me, my real work is to try to live in the presence of God, and to express that presence through my everyday life. Whether I am working on something explicitly religious, like preparing a sermon or writing an email to set up a meeting, I try to do it aware of God acting through me. So my work is not any kind of set of accomplishments that I leave behind me at the office. It's a mindset and an attitude of dedicating every act, no matter how seemingly trivial it may be, to God. And that goes for doing the dishes."

An awareness that God is acting through me is Matt's prayer. It matters less what the activity is that he is doing; it matters more that he does it with a particular mindset.

Prayer and work join hands for Matt: "Throughout the day I talk to God, either in my head or out loud (depending on if others are around!). I try to cultivate a sense of knowing that She is there. I try to pray for a half hour in the morning and evening and squeeze time in on my lunch break . . . but really the most important thing for me is not to have a set time, but rather to just pray as constantly as possible, to make it a habit of life, so that it's ingrained in everything I do. We're creatures of habit, so I try to make it a habit. I just do it, without thinking too much about it or judging or evaluating whether it was good or not."

Just doing it, and not judging or evaluating if we are "good" at prayer allows prayer to accompany us in our actions. Praying in all circumstances cultivates a mindset that allows us to remain in the presence of God.

> *How does God's love abide in anyone*
> *who has the world's goods and sees*
> *a brother or sister in need and yet*
> *refuses to help? 1 John 3:17*

I spent an afternoon with Matt and four others in their early twenties. Their prayer lives inspired me. Of course we pray at work, how else would we make it through the day, they asked. Yes, we believe our actions are prayers. Amy told me that "there is a place for a faith community in my life, but worship as a formal thing does not make as much sense to me as lived prayer does, prayer that you slowly become more aware of in your day-to-day life."

"Does attending church sustain the prayers you express through actions during the week?" I asked. "Sometimes a line from the Lord's Prayer, or a verse from the Psalms, like 'Be still and know that I am God' comes to my mind from church," Matt said. "The priest at my church says 'everyone is welcome at the table' and I try to remember that spirit of acceptance in my interactions at work. I know this is a cliché, but when I am in the middle of my day, asking myself the question 'What would Jesus do?' really helps me."

"When a priest prays about things like photocopier problems, or not letting technology get in the way of people meeting each other in person and other practical things in life, suddenly work and prayer come together for me," Lisa tells me.

Ann works at the Boston's Workers Alliance, which supports the unemployed and underemployed, many with criminal records, in finding work. She helps people write résumés and cover letters, working in a storefront office that is small and very noisy. "I find myself praying for solitude and peace—I see a story emerge on a résumé, talking one to one with someone, and I begin to see God moving in their lives over hard times." Ann's work environment causes her to pray for her own safety. "I know I am supposed to love my neighbor as myself, but I am also scared in the office at times and so I pray for them to find jobs *and* I pray for my own safety." Her prayer is practical, and she keeps a prayer for the workplace on her desk and glances at it during the day. This is an excerpt from it:

> *May God give a blessing on this place,*
> *God bless it from roof to floor,*
> *From wall to wall, from end to end,*
> *From its foundation and in its covering.*
> *All evil be banished,*
> *All disturbance cease,*
> *Captive spirits freed.*

God's spirit alone
Dwell within these walls.

May God's will be found here,
And may there be peace between all
* people who work here.*

Going to church helps Ann see her actions at work as prayers. "I love communion, I always have, but this year it has meant even more. I work in a pretty dangerous area, so I am often holding onto the strength of communion, for Christ to supply the strength he wants me to have to do this work." For Ann, receiving the presence of God in bread and wine is something she recalls in the middle of a workday, and remembering that close physical communion with God gives her strength. Ann and her friends have developed a texting system. They send advice or a comforting word to each other through a text and find that it makes a big difference in a tough workday.

"I don't use a prayer book, but I take a prayer we say with me, it goes something like: 'Before God all hearts are open, all desires known and no secrets are hid.' I love that. I also say simple things like: 'Lord, help.' In my work, when I take on the role of truth teller, I draw on stories I hear in church from the prophets. Like when I don't know what to say, I think of Moses and his courage and story helps me."

Tom worked for an insurance firm. It wasn't enough. He felt an insistent urge to do something different, something that "made a difference." He had financial responsibilities for his growing family of four children and tried to talk himself out of making any professional changes. After a sermon that encouraged Tom to pray about the things he really cared about, he began to pray about his work, about his uncertain future. Praying gave him the courage to change directions. As Tom began to pray about his uncertainty, his vocation emerged.

> *I pray daily, seeking perspective about what is important. What is God's will for me, for us? What should we be doing with our lives? Prayer was part of the reason that I ran for elected office and won. My daily prayers help me as a public servant, keeping me aware of my own shortcomings, humble before God and my brothers and sisters. Prayer also invokes empathy, reminding me to "love my neighbor as myself."*
>
> *For me, prayer involves reading. While I find it fascinating to read the Koran, the Old Testament, Confucian texts, Buddhist writings, or Taoist aphorisms, I gravitate toward the New Testament for inspiration and guidance. Jesus' teachings speak to me:*
>
> - *Judge no one.*
>
> - *Hear the word of God and receive it; do not let the word get choked by deceitfulness of riches or lust for other things.*

- *Take nothing for your journey save a staff and sandals.*
- *Render unto Caesar what is Caesar's, and unto God what is God's.*
- *Whoever shall save his life shall lose it and whoever shall lose his life for my sake shall save it.*
- *What shall it profit a man if he shall gain the whole world but lose his own soul?*

How much time and energy do we devote to our day jobs, the ones that make us money? Can we conservatively say ten hours a day? That leaves about six or seven hours of waking time for everything else. Breakfast fits in there, errands, dinner, putting the kids to bed, reading the news, it all gets gobbled up pretty quickly. Is there enough time for prayer and reflection?

I consider what Jesus did and try to emulate him. As a public servant, I receive inspiration from his example.

- *He healed the sick.*
- *He fed the hungry and the poor.*
- *He spoke out against hypocrites.*
- *He upbraided the moneychangers in the temple.*
- *He responded to questions with questions.*
- *He prayed.*

If time for God is getting choked, it helps to look at emulating Jesus each day as a prayer. With my daily prayer, there are no epiphanies, no flashes of light, no voices coming out of the clouds. The point is the uncertainty. The point is the struggle, the constant attempt to be good and faithful, but to always know that we are human, and always somewhat unsure. And that's what makes us who we are, flawed individuals failing and succeeding, stumbling and achieving every day. No matter how hard we try, we cannot break free of our own fragile, fallible humanity. Think of Simon Peter, perhaps closer to Jesus than any other: he was so earnestly faithful, and yet so tragically human. But God remains there for us in prayer, and God continues to love us.

Am I ready to love my neighbors as Jesus loved the sinners, the lame, the lepers, the simple, the uneducated, the unwashed? That's the group that he ultimately helped. He gave sight to the blind, he healed the sick, he fed the hungry. He gave hope and optimism to those who had so little.

Perhaps all those forgotten and discarded souls that Jesus helped were blessed with the spirit of goodness. Perhaps our role in life is to seek out and find that goodness within others?

I am fortunate to be an elected representative of 40,000 people in Massachusetts. In doing my job every day, I pray. It causes me to consider how those of us in public service should spend our time. For example, we could spend days, months, years rewriting the tax code to help those who are already wealthy. Or we could try to end poverty in our cities. We could speak out against violence. We could provide food stamps for the hungry, jobs for the jobless, and public transportation and child care so the working poor can work. We could help immigrants integrate into our society by helping them find work, shelter, or a supportive community. We could provide assistance and hope to those who, through no fault of their own, were born into unfortunate circumstances.

Jesus said "he that believeth in me, the works that I do shall he do also, and greater works than these shall he do." So when we hear some "radical" voice saying that we shouldn't be at war in Iraq, bear Jesus in mind. When we notice protesters with placards saying "Greed is NOT good," don't brush them aside as if they were lunatics. When we hear inner-city community groups ask the government for more funding so that they can support local health clinics to heal the sick, don't whine about taxes being raised. Put these voices in perspective with Jesus's radical message. Ask whether today's voices are trying to emulate Jesus.

When I pray, I take comfort in the struggle and put myself in the shoes of others as a way of seeking the goodness within them. What fruit does imagining myself in someone else's shoes bear? Imagine, for example, that we are homeless not because of a lack of personal responsibility, but because of a mental illness, which we battled against and tried to push aside and prayed for guidance about, but against which we are now losing the battle. We pray to get our lives back in order.

Or we are Cambodian, former refugees, now living in Lowell, Massachusetts, with a son who is spending too much time with a bad group and was knifed to death over a puerile argument about a stolen iPod. No one had the money to buy one, because we, the parents of the community, can only find jobs that pay a paltry wage.

We can imagine that we are parents raising our beloved children in the inner city and dragging them to church because it is the one stable source of community and hope in a downtrodden and forgotten neighborhood with crime and poverty staring us in the face.

Prayer is not about guilt or motivation from guilt. That's not the point. Prayer is about hope, and the future, and opportunity, and making a positive difference. Prayer offers me guidance in my work as a public servant. It then becomes my actions.

We can imagine a city in which the poor can reach out for assistance and receive it because government leaders have the courage to support programs to lift them up and give them opportunities.

We can imagine an inner-city parish expanding, growing, and providing a common ground for neighbors to bond with neighbors, where day care is provided, and where job training is offered, where mothers can find hope and where fathers can find support and children can read and learn and do their homework and be safe.

We can imagine a business where leading executives are only paid ten times (instead of 400 times) the salary of the lowest-paid worker. A business that pays its employees a living wage that allows them to save for college or to provide new books for their children.

We can imagine schools where teachers are paid appropriately, and are given the opportunity and training and infrastructure to change, improve, and strive for excellence.

We can imagine a country where the sense of service toward the common good outweighs the selfishness of the powerful, where justice outweighs discrimination, where peace and prosperity and progress abound. I can imagine all this when I pray.

Every day, we can pray to seek goodness in

*others until we find God's spirit within them.
And when we do, we may find God's joy here
on this earth. That is worth the effort it takes
to pray and to act.*

At a recent conference, the speaker—a leader
in the national church—talked about changing the
way the church does things to creatively adapt to the
world we live in. Her medium was part of her message, a large screen with beautiful photos spread out
before us, and music as well as tapes of the voices
of social leaders she quoted. Her lecture's message,
through multimedia, was that the church does not
belong to the clergy; the clergy belong to the people
who come to church and pay the bills. The theological education, pastoral support, and spiritual inspiration required to make their lives in the world a
prayer is the work of the parish church. The issues
we face outside the walls of the church can be
addressed within the church, providing opportunity
for people to grapple with the moral and political
dilemmas they face each day and see them reflected
upon in light of Jesus' teachings.

When a lawyer argues a case in a courtroom
or a parent comforts a child, when a postal worker
greets the next in line and a teacher helps a strug-
gling student—these actions can be experiences of
prayer. We practice the presence of God continuously, in all we do and say. We find what fosters a
mindset of continuous prayer and we keep at it. We
practice. We don't achieve anything when we pray.

We are not trying to pray perfectly, or peacefully. We are not trying to make something sacred that feels mundane. We are doing what we do and offering it to God and to God's purposes for us and for those we encounter.

Peter's prayers were in the form of actions he took, offering his work as a realtor to build a school for low- income children. Through Peter's work he developed a deeper faith—in response, he went looking for the support of a church.

❧

My work life has always centered in real estate. My father founded an insurance company in 1957. He started out by providing janitorial and maintenance services, built a brokerage firm, and eventually purchased buildings in the posh Beacon Hill and Back Bay neighborhoods of Boston, Massachusetts.

Everything changed when my father suffered a massive brain aneurysm, slipped into a coma, and died five days later. He was 66. I was immediately running the family business. I had no choice. There was so much work to do I was too busy to grieve.

Months later I was stopped in a long queue of traffic at an intersection close to the hospital where my father had passed away. There was a knock on my car window. Another motorist had gotten out of his car to ask me if I was "all right?" I responded yes, and then he said to me, "Have faith." As he walked away, I looked into the rear view mirror and was startled to see that my face was wet with tears. I will never forget that stranger.

My career in real estate enabled me to hear a call from God. It came from one of God's messengers who asked me to help him launch a school for low-income kids in the inner city. Joe brought years of teaching experience at a school with a similar mission. "They don't believe they can do the work, but sometime, usually in the first year, they have an epiphany and realize that they can." Epiphany School was created. God was at work in this moment.

Many people have worked to build and sustain Epiphany School, but in many instances, the clear provider and solution to our needs was not hard work, or planning, or even money; it was faith and prayer.

We accept boys and girls from low-income households in Boston into the fifth grade through a lottery system. We enter into a partnership with their caregiver(s) and provide a truly innovative learning community. Students attend Epiphany 12 hours each day, eleven months a year. They advance to the next grade only by reaching defined academic, behavioral, and social benchmarks. Epiphany is a resource center for solving life problems for our students and families. Upon graduation, we provide high school placement support for our graduates and often financial aid. Two graduates will finish college this spring and return to Epiphany as intern teachers in the fall.

From the beginning, Epiphany's central problem was real estate—where would we find a permanent and appropriate home? We looked at nearly 100 sites over 18 months, and on three occasions, we were very close, only to have doors shut. The perfect property— an old, cold storage warehouse on nearly an acre of land—came on the market—and we grabbed it.

We had to carefully demolish the warehouse, as it was about to fall down. We made disastrous mistakes, and were forced to find a new builder at the eleventh hour. No matter: our faith strengthened, as did our resolve. We poured foundations for Epiphany's schoolhouse and less than six months later our first day of classes began.

This is what prayer in action can do. Epiphany believes that every person who comes to our school—student, teacher, caregiver, graduate, visitor, or community resident—is sacred.

My journey with Epiphany has brought me closer to what I am called to do by God. I've been asked to organize and lead the school in direction and formation, aided by people far more experienced and talented than I. I've become part of the school community, as a tutor and a volunteer teacher. I even met my wife at Epiphany, while we were building the schoolhouse, and proposed to her on the very same spot. This year, I teach fifth and eighth graders verbal skills, from recited poems to mock high school interviews and most rewarding of all, I help eighth graders prepare their sermons for weekly chapel.

Epiphany's financial model is perhaps more audacious than its mission. Our school is tuition-free. We receive contributions to fund our operations and need to raise more than $2 million annually to operate our extensive program. Each cent is ruthlessly guarded. If we paid the brigade of over-qualified volunteers who help us each week a fair wage, it would be far higher. None of our funding comes from public sources; 65 percent is given by individuals, 30 percent by foundations, and the remainder by businesses and churches. Epiphany needed my help in *raising funds. My work and faith have come closer together, even in raising money.*

Summer time for urban youth is a dangerous time. Many of our students experience idle, hot, summer days. A bad decision or unwittingly getting caught up in an event can completely derail their lives. Epiphany students have active, meaningful summers so that what begins in the school year progresses in our summer program.

Through my work with Epiphany, my faith is growing deeper. In response, I had to find a church to join. I wanted to be part of a community that shared the values that were growing in my life. I will always remember my priest preaching about the need to beat down the mountains between us in the suburbs and those in the city to create a verdant valley connecting us. I know that this can happen. Will we ever have earth as it is in heaven, as the Lord's Prayer prays? I don't know, and I'm sure it sounds wildly idealistic, but if we can marry our faith to some meaningful extent with our actions in the world, there is a chance.

The loss of my father opened up paths for me to build up and live out my faith. God has a purpose for me, and helped me respond to this loss to not only find peace, but meaning and direction, by bringing my prayer to work with me.

Peter's prayer takes the form of action. His faith community motivated him, as he was supported by the affirmation that prayer in action was as authentic as prayers said in the quiet of a chapel.

3

PRAYER
IN THE BODY

*And here we offer and present unto
    Thee, O Lord,
Ourselves, our souls and bodies
To be a reasonable, holy and living
    sacrifice . . .*

—Holy Eucharist I
Book of Common Prayer (p. 336)

WHEN I FOLDED my hands to pray in church, my white gloves were too small. The taut cloth created little hammocks between each finger. I was told to sit with my hands folded because it helped fidgets like me whose squirming distracted others. I crawled beneath the pew to chase after a bulletin that slid out of my hymnal, and if I was quiet I could lie beneath the pew on the cool, smooth floor and stretch out. Men wore shiny dress shoes and thin socks, and women had sheer hose and heels on. Children's feet swung back and forth, unable to reach the floor; their shiny dress shoes cute as a doll's with lacy anklets turned over on small chubby legs. I couldn't wait to be old enough to babysit.

I didn't come to church for God. I came for the people, the fun, and the food. It wasn't that I never talked to God, I just waited until no one else was around. I wondered what life would be like if I lived with the moms and dads in the pews in front of me. Some of them would touch their children with affection during church, rubbing their back or holding the little hand in their big hand and massaging tiny finger muscles. Other families sat with space between them as if they didn't know each other; each person held their own hymnbook, like they had not come in the same car. Another family overlapped limbs as if they were familiar extensions of each other: legs entwined, heads leaning on the other's shoulder, a torso covering the lap of another, they grabbed elbows, snuggled close, pulled a head close to their mouth to whisper in an ear. These families let children too old to suck their thumb do it anyway, caressing the corner of a sibling's sweater as a stand-in blanket.

Women who wore matching shoes and purses intrigued me. I imagined entire closet shelves dedicated to matching brown, red, blue, and beige shoes and bags. When I heard the snap of a purse opening, I peeked over the top of the pew to see what was inside. Some purses were stuffed with notes and trash and little books and a hairbrush with hair in it and a plastic case for lipstick. Sometimes a child got a slap on the leg or a pinch behind the arm from a parent who intended this discipline to take place in secret. When a child's squeal gave the parent away, I worried what would happen in the privacy of the family car and hoped the parent would forget about it by then.

The choir sang from the balcony where the organist sat on the bench to play and direct, at the same time moving his head like a conductor's wand. I sat backwards in my pew in order to watch them as they sang. Some voices stuck out instead of blending in and I would stare at the chorus of faces until I figured out who it was. I wondered how old I had to be to wear the nylon robes that zipped up the front, and why the women's robes had thick white collars and the men's were plain blue.

Sermons were my favorite part. I learned (from watching grown-ups) to check the watch on my dad's tan, hairy wrist to see what time it was when the preacher started. People looked up at the pastor with interest giving a slight nod of "yes" as he spoke. If they drifted to sleep, or got out a pen and made a grocery list on their bulletin, or their head fell forward, I felt embarrassed for him and wished I could make a signal like baseball players did to tell him to stop talking.

I could tell when the preacher believed what he was telling us to believe. That was the mark of a good sermon. Sometimes he expected us to believe something it didn't seem like he believed. Then people got out mints or unwrapped hard candy and played hangman or tic-tack-toe on the back of the pledge envelope in the pew rack.

Once a tall guest preacher with red hair and freckles dressed up in a brown cape and shouted like he was at a ballgame: "Jesus, Son of David, have mercy on me." He yelled it three times, each time more loudly than the time before, which he said was what happened in the Bible story. People looked down at their shoes and opened their bulletins for no reason. I sensed adult anxiety in the sanctuary, as if our preacher was breaking a volume rule someone forgot to tell him about.

When Grandma opened her white leather bible (which she brought from home, full of notes, bookmarks, and pink and yellow highlights) to the Psalms, I knew the sermon was dying a slow death. She told us there was always something to learn from a sermon. Unlike Grandpa, she never said a bad word about the pastor. Grandpa rarely went to church, but that didn't stop him from making fun of pastors he didn't even know. He didn't think it was a real job to do what they did. "Some people need church more than others," he would say, quoting Henry David Thoreau, while filling his pipe with tobacco and getting up for our walk in the woods that followed Sunday dinner.

When I turned 12 years old, I didn't go upstairs to church anymore. I babysat in the nursery. The top half of the nursery door swung open so that parents could hand me their child without children already in the nursery crawling away. There were some really cool young parents who dressed their babies and toddlers in cute outfits. I loved to watch parents hold hands or put their arms around each other as they left the nursery and went upstairs to church. I couldn't wait to be in love and get married and have children and go to church like I was on a date.

A really cute dad with a tan face, white teeth, dark hair, and blue eyes carried his daughter in a yellow dress to the nursery door and told me that the only time he and his wife sat quietly together all week was in church. "Thank God you take care of the children so we can sit together." I wanted to marry someone exactly like him.

Standing at the nursery door, I rested my clip-board on the half-door shelf and wrote in my best penmanship, taking notes about the child's needs. I wrote the name of each child on masking tape three times and tore three nametags off, putting one on the baby's back, one on their bottle, and the third on their diaper bag. I was told to let the mom and dad see that I put it on the correct bag and bottle and child before they left. Working in the nursery was the Lord's work. We were told not to take money for it, but I loved it when I got paid. I knew it was wrong to pay more attention to the children whose parents gave me quarters that they were supposed to put in the offering plate. But I couldn't help it.

Some parents (the best ones) came down from church to claim their child while the organ played the loud closing hymn. Others took advantage of us and left us stuck with their kids and went to coffee hour, picking up their child when coffee hour was nearly over and half the parking lot was empty. The plates full of things we never got at home: choco-late-covered graham crackers, white powdered sugar donuts, and store-bought yellow coffee cakes with raspberry filling topped with squiggly lines of white icing were left with only crumbs.

I talked with God outside of church more than in church. My most fervent prayer was prayed in the back seat of the station wagon on the drive to the dentist. I sat next to the window and put my head between my knees in order to concentrate and prayed with all my might not to have a cavity. I loved candy and ice cream and cakes and pies and cookies. (We weren't allowed to drink soda pop.) I knew sweets would give me cavities, but I prayed for a miracle. I shuddered at the horrid burned smell and piercing sound of the drill and was afraid of the long needle of Novocain which hurt so much more than a bee sting, filling my mouth with that terrible taste and thick numbness. I didn't expect God to erase holes in my teeth caused by all the sugar I ate. But I knew miracles sometimes happened, so I prayed for one. I promised God I would be nice to everyone in my family, everyone at church, and all my friends, and stop eating candy if only this once I had no cavities. Even if no miracle happened, I prayed because I did not want to face the dentist alone. I memorized a verse from Psalm 23 and repeated it to myself: "Yea though I walk through the valley of the shadow of death, thy hand is with me" (KJV).

I needed God at school too. I wrote prayers to God in my journal, starting in fourth grade. I prayed about everything. I prayed before my audition that I would make the choir. I prayed for invitations to slumber parties. I prayed for a boy to ask me to dance, to make it into aqua teens, to help my parents say yes to letting me do more things. I didn't keep the boring details from God. I thanked God for dinner when we had homemade applesauce and fried pork chops rolled in cracker crumbs, for new white boots, and my first purse. I turned to God when I felt alone, when I was angry and wasn't allowed to be angry, and when I needed help.

I needed the particular kind of friend I learned Jesus was; life was lonely and confusing when I was 14 years old. I needed help leaving summer camp and saying good-bye to my first boyfriend, Chuck, to return to my family. I asked Jesus to go with me to my first year in a big, scary high school. When Chuck got on one bus and I got on another, Jesus had already started to make a big difference to me: I didn't feel so alone.

My favorite stories about Jesus are the ones where he is doing things in his body. I could imagine him as a real person rowing in a boat, making a charcoal fire and grilling fish, walking on roads, sitting at a well, turning over tables, looking up and finding Zacchaeus in a tree and telling him to come down to go to dinner together. I liked God in Jesus with a physical life in a body.

Athletes look heavenward and make the sign of the cross, or fold their hands, or close their eyes in prayer before their sport. Runners talk of their minds clearing as they take to the road, or a path through the woods bringing a sensation of sacred peace and holiness to their body and mind. Dancers share the spiritual connection they experience when their mind stops thinking about the moves and they feel the music inside, transported by movement into praise, into dancing as a form of prayer.

Everyone benefits from Steve's love for dancing, as he extends a hand, inviting people to dance at the end of a day of meetings. The talking is finally over and, after dinner, we start up the music and move. Steve writes:

My public debut as an ecstatic dancer did not go well. I had invited a girl onto the floor at my first high school dance. When I started to move to the music in the way that I did in my room at night with the radio on loud, a look of panic came over her face as she slowly backed away from me.

I felt much more at home many years later in worship at an Amahoro gathering outside Kampala, Uganda. The opening song of praise began and, naturally, we danced. We danced from song to song, in the rhythms of tribes and nations. We danced in circles. We danced around the room. We danced with our hips shaking and our hands waving and enormous smiles breaking our faces. I thought, this is more like it.

Dancing is my favorite way of not thinking. The will and knowing come not from my head, but from somewhere at the other end of my spine. I don't listen to music coming from outside. I focus on the place inside that hears the music as movement and moves me.

I like tuning in to something alive within me that is not in my control and that shows up in the world in surprising and delightful ways. I like doing that in my room at night with the radio loud. I like it on the dance floor at wedding receptions, just please could I have it in church?

Going to church is like going on a run, my 24-year-old son tells me. He puts it off, he doesn't want to go, he finds excuses and procrastinates, but when he goes, he never regrets it. He loves the feeling he has when walking out of church just as he loves finishing a run. He feels whole in body, mind, and spirit. This spiritual dimension within the experience of athletic training and competing is captured by Maddy, a cross-country skier.

At the finish line of every ski race, God is waiting for me.

He is not who I think about as I joke with my teammates, trying to alleviate pre-race jitters, and He rarely surfaces in my thoughts as I struggle to keep up with competitors five, ten, fifteen, or fifty kilometers at a time. For meters, miles, and sometimes hours on end, I ski until my body reaches its limit. With legs burning and lungs screaming, I block out the pain and try to push harder and go faster, harder and faster, harder and faster, until I lunge across that red line painted in the snow, physically spent.

There is no greater feeling than this.

Emptied of energy stores, emotion, and thought at the end of a race, I contain nothing but God. The feeling is best when I collapse, panting, on the ground just over the line. Knowing I used up every last resource in my body means that I performed at my best and held nothing back. The snow on which I lay is cold, the bells and the cheering crowd are loud. I am hungry, thirsty, and exhausted. But for a precious few minutes, I feel as if I am completely empty and my body is light, floating on air. In a word, I feel Peace.

After a childhood of Catholic school and daily Mass, my husband might agree with Thoreau's sentiment that "some people don't need as much church as others." One day, after a bicycle ride he said to me, "When I die I want my ashes scattered over the beautiful fields and meadows, hills and country roads I biked by today." Bicycling is a form of prayer for Michael. In his words:

I was riding my bicycle recently and sat up, balancing on the seat and lifted my arms into the air and let out a loud "whoop." At that moment I was in the presence of God. How did I know that? How could I say that God was present with me then? Because of how I felt. My spirit was uplifted because the road was smooth and freshly paved. The sky was gloriously blue and sun filtered through the brilliant green trees of early summer. My legs felt strong, stronger than they normally did, and stronger than they should have felt for someone about to turn 56. I looked up at the sky. I looked down at my legs. I felt a great sense of energy and peacefulness at the same time. This was a prayer; if not a prayer, a gift from God. I remember the experience of joy and excitement like this happening every day as a child. It didn't take much: a booming shower of fireworks overhead, a large black snake skimming rapidly across a lawn with my brothers and me in hot pursuit, a ride in the back of a pickup along a dirt road. Joy was everywhere, a daily occurrence. As I grow older, occasions of great joy are more widely spaced. The presence of God comes at unexpected times: a piece of music touches something inside me, or the pleasure of one of my children's accomplishments or actions, it might be a sermon, or a swim in a lake on a summer evening. It is hardly something I can plan for. Seeking it doesn't reliably lead to finding it, but I can most reliably find joy on a bicycle. I understand prayer as a complete immersion into something without restraint or distraction compromising my ability to pay attention for an extended period of time without interruption. Prayer is the gift of being able to immerse myself fully into something and have that thing occupy my mind and my body, consciously and unconsciously. This is prayer for me. It happens most clearly in my body on a bicycle when the presence of God is a pure and tangible heat and the world and all its distractions slip away. I am reduced to breathing, a precise aware-ness of the strength in my legs, the hill up ahead that I overtake by counting the rota-tions of my pedal strokes, the flow of moving by meadows and lakes or through the trees on a forested single-track trail. These are times when I feel alive, aware, focused, and at prayer.

The summer I was 17, I worked as a camp counselor at a Young Life camp in British Columbia where tall mountains soared high and plummeted deep into the sea like the fjords of Norway. I wrote in my journal: "The mountains here are majestic, I have never seen anything like them. Looking at them is not enough. I want to climb them or eat them, or somehow take in their beauty." The Canadian poet Anne Carson became so enchanted by a copy of *The Lives of the Saints* as a child that she tried to eat it.

The first time I knelt at an altar rail to receive communion I knew I had found a way to connect with God. Leaving my pew, standing up and going to the altar, opening my hands and having bread and then wine given to me to take into my body, I felt small, not ashamed or worthless, but safe, cared for, and in awe. Communion was like finding my way inside a mountain or eating a book. It satisfied my longing for God at a level deeper than my thoughts. Walking forward and kneeling, then opening my hands to be given bread and wine didn't happen because I was good or bad. It wasn't a reward for hard work or a punishment for mistakes I'd made. I couldn't be good enough or bad enough to deserve communion. It didn't make sense really, and I liked that, too. The food was offered, not to fill me up, but to feed my soul, the eternal part of me that would never die where God lived now. None of it was about me, or dependent upon me, it was an encounter with God in church. Everything stopped. The minister quit talking and we got up from our seat and it was a way of getting closer to God than my ideas about God would allow. God came into my body. The sacrament helped me stop explaining God. It didn't try to bring God down to my level. I moved into a mystery that I'd never figure out. The empty feeling I often had went away. I didn't come to communion to show God the good parts, the shiny dressed up parts of me, I came to say thank you.

When I teach communion class to children, I bring orange juice and a plain donut. They have no trouble understanding the mystery of the words that transform the food into soul food. Is this enough for breakfast, I ask? "No, we need more donuts!" they reply. The piece of donut and the sip of juice feed the part of us that is hungry for God, not hungry for breakfast. We eat in a circle together to feed our soul for the week ahead.

Communion is a bodily sacrament. It is physical. We come together to take in the presence of Jesus. It goes beyond hearing one of his teachings; we step into communion with him in our body.

There were two elements in the redesign of our worship space that I wanted a hand in, and they involved the body and the sacraments: the way we received communion and the way we celebrated baptism. Our altar allowed for 12 people to come forward and kneel behind a rail facing the priest and the altar. I wanted people to be able to look across a circle as they stood or knelt for communion. To witness a face filled with joy, or tears, a child happy to be part of the circle at the altar. The sacrament was not between the priest and people alone, it belonged to the community. We stand or kneel, we taste the wine and bread, we feel the breeze coming in the window, or watch the rain, we hear the words. Communion is a sacrament for body and soul, and the altar shaped our experience of this outward act that brought the inward grace we came to receive.

The old baptismal font at the back of the nave was covered in plastic; bulletins, acolyte robes, and coats piled on top of it. When we redesigned our sanctuary, we moved it, creating a space for Baptism to be central to our community identity. Placed under a skylight, morning light beamed on the marble font now centered in the sanctuary entrance. We walked through the waters of Baptism each time we entered the sanctuary and were reminded of God's love for us. No bad week, no untimely death, no 9/11, no divorce or infertility or sorrow, no triumphant accomplishment or dream come true would separate us from our first identity: God's own, loved and forgiven and washed in the waters of baptism to belong forever to the communion of saints.

❦

Laura's is a story of prayer in the body. She writes:

Monks are awake at 3:00 a.m., like me. Cloaked in black, they sit in straight-back stalls and chant the psalms. A solemn, serious prayer. Wrapped in my bathrobe, I rock in my grandmother's chair and whisper lullabies. A soft, soothing prayer.

Awakened by a newborn's cry, not abbey bells, I feel miles away from a monastery. But as I nurse the baby, my thoughts drift to the men whose calling wakes them in the night like mine does. Our prayers are ancient, our songs well worn and set the rhythm of our days. A mother of two, I am no monk. But I have learned that my work is theirs, and our work is prayer.

Before my name became "mama," I thought

prayer was a quest to be conquered. If I were just more disciplined, or read more books, or made more time for silence, then I could find the inner peace I craved. Shoving aside the mess of life's distractions was surely the only way to inch closer to God. I lined shelves with a rainbow of books on prayer. I dabbled in ancient wisdom, tried every latest craze. I was convinced that if I could find the right technique, my life would transform into a dreamy, Zen-like bliss. I would become a perfect prayer. Then in a single shocking instant, a nurse scooped the slippery, screaming baby into my shaking arms. I kissed the top of his warm, slimy head and whispered as the delivery room bustled around me: thank you, God, O thank you God. I didn't know this birthday would change my prayer life, too.

At first I tried to cram old prayer habits into my new life as a mother. But like stuffing my post-baby body into pre-baby jeans, it just didn't fit, no matter how hard I shoved. I was too tired for morning prayer, too cranky for evening meditation. The baby spit up all over my book of psalms one night, and I hurled it across the room in frustration.

For months I fumed. In the dark before dawn I would lie in bed and dream of starting my morning with a sun salutation and some scripture. A prayer and a poem, a cup of tea and a bit of conversation with God. But my fantasies were always interrupted by the shrieks of a hungry baby wailing to be fed, heaps of laundry pleading to be folded, and a sink full of dishes screaming to be scrubbed. My life as a new mother seemed dirty and demanding and utterly devoid of prayer.

But as dust collected on the bookshelves and the candles sat unlit, I started to settle into the work of mothering—one boy, then two. And as the months slipped by, I began to see, surprisingly, how full of prayer this new work was. I found myself meeting God in unexpected moments. A grin from a baby delighted with his own toes, a quiet cuddle with a cranky toddler. If I slowed for a second while caring for their constant needs, I could breathe into the gratitude of the gift I'd been given: two small boys to love and teach and help grow.

When I cupped my toddler's face in my hands, peanut butter smeared around his mouth, I prayed to God in a way that felt real: Bless him. Help me. Thank you. And when I strapped my baby in his spit-up-caked car seat and wiped salty traces of tears from his eyes, I felt God reaching right back: Love them. Forgive you. Find me.

Much to my surprise, I didn't need a quiet chapel filled with candles to pray. I could pray in a laundry-strewn living room with a colorful crunch of Legos underfoot. And my meditation didn't need smoky incense dancing up towards heaven. Prayer smelled sweeter with milky baby breath drooling down my shoulder. Caring for these boys, day after day, proved that prayer didn't have to be discipline or structure or silent. It could be sloppy and scattered, but it was still speaking with God. The Spirit I'd sought in the cool dark of cathedrals was the same I met in the sticky, sweaty chaos of life with my boys. Motherhood taught me that microwaving leftovers for dinner is prayer. That sitting up all night with a feverish, coughing child is prayer. That throwing up on the drive to work every morning for nine months is prayer. Whenever I lifted myself out of selfish desires—for a life with more sleep, less laundry, fewer interruptions—I met God. Parenting taught me how the ordinary could be holy, how even the dirty can lead to the divine.

My work as a parent is neither glitzy nor glamorous. Wiping snotty noses and washing stinky diapers. Scrubbing food off the floor and crayon marks off the wall. Dealing with teething and temper tantrums and toys in every corner. But this work is prayer, too. Wiping noses is prayer for healing. Changing diapers is prayer for comfort. Calming tantrums is prayer for peace. When I put two feet on the cold floor each morning to tend the ones I love (and the chores I hate), it is prayer.

The work of love done for them through God. Done for God through them.

Settling into my rocking chair to nurse the baby once more, I wander back to the monks in the monastery. I used to believe that real prayer was reserved for the religious—the holy few who gave their lives to God. But I have learned from a boy with a mop of golden curls and a baby with dark, laughing eyes what I hungered to know about relationship and growth, surprise and wonder, loving and listening. In chasing my children I glimpse the God I seek. My prayer life today is messier than I'd like to admit. Petitions snuck in between diaper changes, praises sung after endless rounds of ABCs. The work of caring for little ones has become my daily practice of living in the presence of God. A mother of two, I am no monk. I thank God that it was motherhood that made my life prayer.

I often ask people who have stepped away from the church if they miss anything about going to church. What every person tells me is that they miss belonging to a community. They want to know and be known by people in a faith community, to belong and feel part of its life, and the second thing they tell me is that they want to experience God for themselves in a living relationship that is a reality in their life. As I watch the popularity of yoga spread across our culture, and practice it myself, I believe there are several things the church can learn from its practice.

I am not looking for a new religion in yoga; I am looking to expand my practice of prayer to include my body. Christian tradition teaches that we are living temples, sacred vessels that the Holy Spirit dwells in. The incarnation of God into a human body and historical life is an invitation to honor our body as a vehicle for prayer. The Christian tradition respects the body, intellectually, as a place where God dwells. It is a sound theological idea in Christianity, but not a practice. I came to yoga in need of a practice that honored the body and used it as a vehicle for prayer. The word yoga means union. The practice unites the mind, body, and spirit; it is a practice of prayer that offers what so many people seek, a way to experience the Spirit as a living reality in their life that includes the training and discipline of the mind and care and respect for the body.

Growing up in the church, I learned to fear, even to hate, my body. It was my lesser part; my body was a problem to solve, it needed to be reined in, kept quiet, kept hidden. I was taught to judge my body harshly, critically, and to remain distant from it because it would lead me to do bad things, like eat too much or drink alcohol or have sex. The body was not something to listen to or give thanks for; it was to be disciplined, restrained, and ignored.

Two long, winding lines of people with rolled mats, water bottles, and comfortable clothes wait at the check-in desk on Sunday morning at the yoga studio half a block down the street from church. We turn sideways to edge our way through the crowd coming out of class to find a place to unroll our mats on the smooth bamboo floor. The instructor asks people to make room for three more mats in a room already crowded. In the front of the room candles are lit, and there is a sweet odor. Some people are meditating, others are quietly talking to friends. We are wearing tights, and t-shirts, shorts, and tank tops; there is no dress code and no one cares what someone else is wearing. People are thin, and fat, tall and short, black, brown, gay, straight, male, female, Asian, Latino/Latina, white. An older man lies on his back, his eyes covered with a little beanbag and a blanket over him. A young woman is standing on her head in the corner. You can take any posture you want, or none at all, as you leave the world outside and come into the practice of yoga.

I was attracted to yoga for years but never made time for it until my daughter left for college eight years ago. I practiced silent meditation, but never made time to practice postures. Yoga has become a form of prayer for me, an offering of myself to God. The training and discipline of my mind and body increases the space I have in my life for God, for myself, and for other people.

The practice of yoga has given me a place to heal a relationship with my body that was adversarial and critical. I wanted to learn how to give thanks for, accept, and even love my body as a gift from God. The practice of yoga as prayer is healing the destructive relationship I learned to have with myself and with my body. Its lessons are being learned by my mind, my body, and my spirit. Yoga is a practice of prayer whose goal is union with God.

Yoga creates and opens space within a person, not as an idea, but as an experience. Just as muscle strength increases with weight-lifting, so it is in yoga: the practice of breathing and holding postures increases flexibility, openness, and strength in muscles, joints, tendons, and bones, and in one's mind and heart. Room is made for God to dwell in my daily life by actually creating space in my body. Yoga is the practice of surrender to God, not as an idea or moral effort, but as a physical practice that increases spiritual awareness.

My teacher says: "Breath is yoga." Breath filled our lungs when we were born and our breath will cease when we die. The breath is the vehicle for transformation in yoga practice. Not as an idea about how to open, lengthen, strengthen, or heal the body, breath provides for the actual physical transformation of the body. Our breath is part of the Living Breath that animates and gives life to the world, it is the Holy Spirit that gives us life.

This morning I did not want to go to yoga. I was up for hours restless in the night, and I awoke feeling irritable. I didn't want to go to yoga like I don't want to pray when I'm angry or feeling down. (Why is it hardest to pray when we need it the most?) I went to yoga anyway. Yoga, like prayer, is not for good or bad moods. It is a practice for life just as prayer is a form of life.

Yoga is a form of prayer for me. When I arrive in a pose that takes mental focus, concentrated breath, and sustained attention: I have to be. I try not to itch or inch my way out of the pose. Staying with the pose increases my ability to endure discomfort. This is how yoga prepares me for living life. When I am uncomfortable during my day, in a traffic jam, annoyed with people, angry at someone, and impatient, I have a resource from my practice that says: "You can do this." When I am asked to hold a pose, and breathe, and want to quit, but don't, that endurance contributes to the inner reservoir available to me when life puts me in a place I don't want to be in. I learn to hold the pose, breathe, and as one teacher puts it, "just deal."

My bishop once told me I had a problem with comparison mind. I knew he was right and tried to stop it; I tried to be content with myself and not compare myself with others in order to feel good about myself. It didn't work until I began to practice it on the mat and physically learn its lesson. Listening to where I was, not comparing myself to the person next to me who started yesterday or the person in front of me who was a seasoned practitioner, was the only way I would grow in the practice. Comparison would get me nowhere, fast. I couldn't break the habit of comparison mind until I learned how useless it is through yoga practice.

Yoga, like prayer, as prayer, is not something

you get good at. You just get better as you practice. Yoga is an infinite practice. One pose is mas-
tered and you see that it leads to another and then
another. There is no mood, or situation, or personal
problem, no life decision, no sadness or happiness
that it does not welcome. The discipline is simply to
do it, as regularly as possible, just like prayer.

The closing pose in yoga practice is relaxed con-
centration. You lie flat on your back with legs and
arms comfortably outstretched, and close your eyes,
gently: corpse pose. The first time I lay in this pose,
the prayer *Into Thy hands I commend my spirit*
floated across my mind. I repeat it each time I end
my practice.

4

PRAYER
IN ART

What is there, truly done,
that is not a prayer?

—Rainer Maria Rilke[1]

---

1   *A Companion to the Works of Rainer Maria Rilke,* E. A. Metzger
and M. M. Metzger, eds. (Rochester, NY: Camden House, 2001), 15.

I N A RECENT radio interview, popular singer and
songwriter Carole King described the process of
writing lyrics and composing music. The inter-
viewer asked her about a particularly well-loved
song she wrote in the late 1960s. Ms. King said: "I
didn't work at the lyrics or discipline myself to finish
the music. The song came right through me."

Art and prayer. We engage in creativity, and art
becomes a medium for prayer. As we create, we participate in creation, participate in the sacred act that
gives God the name Creator. And we pray in art
as we behold it, listen to it, gaze upon it. Through
music, painting, dancing, or poetry, we are led into
the source of all creativity, our Creator. When asked
about his music, the great jazz artist Duke Ellington
said: "Now I can say loudly and openly what I've
been saying on my knees."

Many artists describe themselves as the instrument more than the author of their work. The act of
creating tunes them to an intuitive voice or direction that guides them, aids them, supplies inspiration and discipline. Those moments of inspiration
can then compel us toward faith that something is

being brought into being through the gifts and talents we possess.

Creativity—bringing something into being out of the imagination given to us by God—is a way to pray. A Swedish poet said, "I would like to carve a wooden spoon so plain that people see God." The quality of transcendence in art, its capacity to become more than it appears, infuses artistic endeavor with prayer. My favorite church organist often quotes Augustine when inspiring his choir. "When you sing, you pray twice," he says. The prayer of making music, combined with the words sung, double one's prayer.

Praying with art does not have to be a trip to a museum or concert. Have you listened to a country western tune on the radio that surfaces unfulfilled desires you didn't even know you have? I have! Have you watched a movie or seen something beautiful and, without warning, found a lump in your throat or tears in your eyes? Maybe the song or poem doesn't even seem worthy of your reaction, but there it is. Art has the capacity to enlarge us, reflect who we are, and generate. We sense Someone standing behind the art we witness, speaking through it to us. This transcendent element in art opens it as an avenue for our prayer, mysteriously deepening or widening our connection with God.

Each member of our church board, the vestry, was asked to lead us in prayer at the beginning of our monthly meeting. The month it was Mike's turn, he pulled a book of music from his briefcase and walked over to the grand piano in the room where our meeting took place. Without introduction, he sat down and played a Beethoven sonata. No words, just music. Tired from the day, we stopped talking and became still, not a sound in the room but the piano. We listened, resting in the music. It was beautiful and soothing, and no one wanted Mike to stop playing. The music had lifted our spirits and given us the gift of being together beyond the finances we had to review and decisions we would argue over. Prayer in art.

Music is often the aspect of worship that most clearly speaks to people. Music awakens what sleeps in us in a way that the preached word cannot. It is as if music catches our intellect up short, opening our imagination before we can criticize it or analyze it. It is as if music, perhaps all art, is subversive. It moves us beyond ourselves to God before we can intellectually stop it from happening. The arts come to us as bearers of eternity, reminders we are made in the image and likeness, not of a great big brain, but of a Creator.

A close friend of mine lost her mother and two sisters within a short period of time. People grieve differently. There is not one way to face loss or even a best way. We get through it in ways that are our own, and it helps when others are not judging us. I told myself this, but even so, I worried about my friend. She did not talk about her losses very often or cry over them as I imagined she would need to. One evening we went to a play together. Not too far into the play, I looked over to see her face drenched in tears. She cried during the entire play. As we left, she told me this was when she grieved: at a play, viewing a movie, listening to music; unexpectedly, the art breaks through to her grief and tears wash over her. The healing properties of art are an aspect of its vitality as a form of prayer.

> *God bless the artist and keep them safe,*
> *praise the creator and those who create,*
> *touch the senses, strike the chord*
> *sound the trumpet, praise the Lord.*
>
> —From *God Bless the Artists*[2]

Several years after the Beethoven sonata prayed for us, the building renovations we were discussing at that meeting were complete. The walls of our new parish hall were freshly painted; light streamed into the open space through tall windows on three sides, reflected in pale blond polished floors. I walked alone in the empty room on a weekday afternoon imagining it as an art gallery. I pictured dividers being installed to increase the wall space, and I imagined them hung with pictures. I saw glass-topped tables displaying jewelry, shelves lined with woodcarvings, a poetry corner. I wanted the prayers of creativity I knew to be part of so many people's lives to come inside this beautifully renovated place of prayer, to be seen and enjoyed.

---

2   Phyllis Dewey Houghton, lyrics; Suzzy Roche, music, *Zero Church, Red House Records, 2002.* Used by Permission.

Knowing it would take some persuasion to get people to bring their art to church, I began shamelessly soliciting it months before we transformed our fellowship hall into an art gallery. We hung works from amateur artists, young children, senior members, and every age in between. Jewelers shined silver pieces and set them on blue velvet in the display case a woodworker in the parish made. A corner was set aside for displays of carved wood. Woven baskets were placed on tiered shelves, poetry was framed and mounted on a wall at the entry. One wall was devoted to photography. An exquisite and intricately patterned knit sweater hung against the white wall. At the gallery opening, we served food and drinks and placed flowers on tables around the room. People took turns playing musical pieces on the piano, saxophone, violin, and cello. A guitarist sang and played a piece he wrote himself. That Sunday, our forum between services was a poetry reading and our coffee hours found people enjoying each other's creativity. As we walked around the room, I heard one comment: "I had no idea you . . . painted, sang, photographed, wove, wrote, played." The community shared the creative dimension of their life that most of us had never shared before.

The Sunday after the gallery opening, I welcomed artists to bring to the altar art that could be moved into the sanctuary. We thanked God for the gift of creativity, blessing the artists and their art. Something important happened in our community that day. Blessing the creative impulse given us by

God hallowed the common, amateur creative work of people as a sacred dimension of their life and prayer. New doors of our imagination and our life in the Holy Spirit opened as we honored the prayer that is in art.

Acknowledging the sacred in our creative endeavors and sharing them with each other allowed us to begin to see our creativity as a prayer; the creative potential in each of us emanating from our Creator. The act of creating, of using the imagination, regardless how amateur or professional, brought us to closer union with God, and we were introduced to a new dimension in each other's lives. As we witnessed each other's art, we came to know each other better. A photography display from a trip to Istanbul, a poem, a song, a dance, a wood carving, were shared prayers, expressions of the Creator through our own creativity that opened us to new dimensions in our relationship with God and each other. The prayer of art harnesses creativity from the springs of our life force, our Creator. As Dylan Thomas puts it, God is "the force that through the green fuse drives the flower."

A friend of mine who lost three colleagues in the 9/11 attack attended a U2 concert at Madison Square Garden three months after the tragedy. While the band played a well-known song, the names of all those who died were projected onto a wall. His description of the experience and the connection it forged for those in attendance reminded me of what Celtic Christians call "a thin place": a place where the membrane between this world and the next becomes very thin and the presence of God is deeply felt. Prayer as art.

The poet of the religious imagination, William Blake, said: "I myself do nothing. The Holy Spirit accomplishes all through me." The transcendent nature of artistic creativity is what allows it to share in the language and experience of prayer. Prayer can be practiced as an artist participates in the stream of creative life that emanates from the creativity of Divine life. The psalms tell us "in Thy light we see light."

The writer James Carroll finds "the very act of storytelling, of arranging memory and invention according to the structure of narrative is, by definition, holy"[3]—expressing the way narrative informs his faith, and his faith informs the purpose of writing.

Writer Ron Hansen shares that "church-going and religion were in good part the origin of my vocation as a writer, for along with Catholicism's feast for the senses, its ethical concerns, its insistence on seeing God in all things, and the high status it gave to scripture, drama, and art, there was a connotation in liturgy that story mattered."[4]

---

3   *The Book That Changed My Life: Interviews with National Book Award Winners and Finalists*, Diane Olsen, ed. (New York: Random House, 2002).

4   *A Stay Against Confusion: Essays on Faith and Fiction* (New York: Harper Perennial, 2002), xii.

Perhaps you have had the experience of reading a story or poem that means so much more to you than the words. The words combine to transcend the words, describing something you felt or thought, but never imagined putting into or seeing in words. It may have happened to you while listening to music, or viewing a painting or sculpture: Suddenly there is so much more than the colors and shapes, harmonies or melody lines. The art speaks to us, conveying to us something that had previously been expressionless.

Like Rainer Maria Rilke's poem:

If Only for Once it Were Still[5]

If only for once it were still.
If the not quite right and the why this
could be muted, and the neighbor's
    laughter,
and the static my senses make—
if all of it didn't keep me from coming
    awake—

Then in one last thousandfold thought
I could think you up to where thinking ends.

I could possess you,
even for the brevity of a smile,
to offer you
to all that lives,
in gladness.

---

5   *Rilke's Book of Hours*, 53. Used by permission.

Mary sang in the church choir on occasion, and she always spoke with me following the service. She was shy and had an ethereal quality about her, responding in unique and unpredictable ways to the sermon, music, and liturgy. She experienced the world of faith and the community of our church through a refreshingly different lens. It took a few years before I learned that she was an artist and a professor of fine arts. When we began to solicit art from the parish for our gallery opening, she offered to bring a series of her paintings. They arrived and we hung them on the balcony stairwell wall in the church foyer where they caught light from a two-story window. Mary gave the series as a gift to the church and shared these thoughts on art as prayer.

In the beginning, the decision to become a painter is a leap of faith. It was, indeed, a leap for me. The first big leap of faith was to accept the value of art and more broadly, the value of human culture. When I first saw great paintings, I had a profoundly humbling experience of not knowing. I did know that on some level I was perceiving something transformational, but there was a wide gulf between the object and my ability to penetrate its mysteries. The starting point is curiosity accompanied by trust. My decision to devote my life to painting was fundamentally a decision to choose a particular lens through which to see and filter all the knowledge and experience I could accumulate in one little (for it is brief) life. That particular aperture remains open to the complexity, the diversity, and the mystery at the core of human experience.

I have seen how art connects us, as people, to what is common in our life's journeys—the revelations at the core of shared catharsis and the comfort of shared grief. Art crosses cultural boundaries to unite us, and that is good. Inspiration and comfort reside in that vast community of ideas contained in art books, museums, and sketchbooks. Faith in this collected memory and its concrete ineffability is essential.

Making paintings is a very solitary occupation. The painter enters that solitude willingly, sometimes gratefully and sometimes with dread. Painters are choosing to be alone, a lot. It is in the silence of solitude where uncertainty blooms.

Just for a few moments I want to take you into the studio and describe how faith enters into the daily practice of painting, the effort of making one particular object. Every painting is a separate, discreet journey. It is its own story with its own lovely process of trial and error. Faith in the studio is fundamentally tolerating a state of uncertainty. Imagine the empty blank stare of canvas or paper. You have to start somewhere. The process has to become physical. I start with an idea, a spark, and then I begin to build a surface with paint, the first layer. This demands both focus and physical energy. It takes tenacity to remain in the search, finding a way through the dead ends. The initial idea gives way to the immediacy of the moments of change. Every decision, at this point, takes the painter into uncharted territory. The way forward is unknown and the way back is closing in behind you. The birds have eaten all the crumbs you carefully left to guide you back. After entering the valley of despair and failure, the temptation is to give up. The painter acknowledges that she needs help. To solve the problem she will need resources other than her vulnerable and lonely brain. Enter devotion and reverence, meditative contemplation, filling the mind's eye with effortless awe. At this point, tolerating the doubt and vulnerability I felt was possible with patience and compassion, fruits of my faith, which slowly transformed my fears into a generative force—a new idea, a beautiful possibility. In this moment, there is faith that everything I need in order to proceed is available to me. This feels like a gift of grace, a grace arriving through love and through devotion to the task. Finally, the painting has enough physical body and begins to proclaim itself as a thing apart, discreet and, yes, unknowable.

*There is a very important role in this phys-
ical act for the dynamic relationship between
the comprehensible and the incomprehensible.
The dance is continuous between the two. And
compassion and gratitude are pure energy!
Sometimes, great works of art seem to teeter
on the verge of incomprehensibility, communi-
cating the quaking vulnerability of the artist's
search. I love the teaching of Jesus: lose your
life to save it. It is another expression for a
leap of faith. It also sounds like the thought
that faith precedes understanding.*

*As a painter, the lens is open. Complete
comprehension is not available, so an open
mind is essential. Sparks of insight are accu-
mulated shard by shard, bit by bit. Faith
allows these sparks to coalesce, eventually
becoming embodied in a painting. A painting
comes into being through the dance of intention, accident, and grace. If there is beauty, it
comes from the vibrant connection of matter
and pure energy. The painter knows that the
work is complete when it has moved beyond
her ken. There follows a deep and resonant
gratitude for this gift of grace.*

I flew into Sarasota to meet friends for a long
weekend. Leaving snow and sleet in February, I was
greeted by Florida sunshine and warm temperatures as I walked out of the airport to the car. As
we drove from the airport, one friend insisted on

stopping to see the Chihuly glass exhibit at a local museum. I had heard of, but never seen, his work, and was sure that it was the last thing I wanted to do on a beautiful day with friends I had not seen for years. How exciting could glass blowing be? I'd seen it at the state fair. Overruled, we stopped, bought tickets, and went into the museum.

It was stunning. The colors of glass—just the pure intensity of color—drew me in, enveloped me. The contours of glass were otherworldly but anchored in shapes I knew well: round balls, large seashells, balloons, and varieties of flowers. An entire room was dedicated to a garden installation. Colored glass blown into shapes tall and thin as sea grasses, thick as tree trunks, round as sunflowers, small as dandelions were combined to create a shiny translucent glass garden. I was in a world I'd never been in before. A life-size wooden fishing boat was filled with variously sized, intensely colored glass balls. Simple, familiar: a boat, round balls, but it drew me in. Standing near it, looking into the colors and easy shapes, worlds of adventure and light took my imagination far from the air-conditioned hum of the room.

Music has the same capacity to transport us. Have you noticed the way a piece of music expresses something that you did not think could be expressed? Or the way it connects people across barriers of language, creed, religion, and culture? Music is prayer in its capacity to express our experience often without words, to provide companionship in solitude, to change a mood or express the inexpressible. A friend of mine studied classical music and told me that Mozart found composing was like "taking dictation from on high." Many of us find that music lifts us toward God. The arts and aesthetics satisfy a thirst for the Absolute. Art and Beauty are sacred vehicles, prayers that transport and allow us to transcend our lives through our imagination.

When members of my family are tired or irritable and there are tasks to do, meals to prepare, trash to go out, dishes to wash, or a dog to feed, music eases and sometimes changes a room full of ornery moods. The musical style seems to matter little. Music has power to change an atmosphere, to speak without words, and in its own right, to minister to our experience. Listening to, singing, composing, or performing music becomes an experience of prayer.

Brother Michael McGrath says his experience of art as prayer began with the simple act of entering a museum, surrounded by the awe, majesty, and mystery he felt when he entered the sanctuary of his church on Sunday. "Art and religious faith go hand in hand for me," he writes. "I don't recall a time when I haven't loved to draw or paint . . . art has continuously given me a sense of doing something unique and worthwhile. I see it as a sacred calling, a vocation to coin a Catholic school word. Art is prayer and sacrament."

Art as prayer inspires us, gives us communion with each other, and comforts us. Henri Matisse said that he wanted his paintings to have the effect on a viewer as an easy chair does after a long day. Delight, pleasure, comfort—are all aspects of art as prayer. The words of St. Paul writing to the Romans seem appropriate to describe the energy inside prayer that is expressed in art: "when we don't know how to pray, the Holy Spirit prays for us with sighs and groans too deep for words."

Pope John Paul II wrote this in an encyclical to artists:

> *In order to communicate the message
> entrusted to her by Christ, the church
> needs art. Art must make the percep-
> tible and as far as possible attractive,
> the world of the spirit, the invisible, of
> God. It must translate into meaningful
> terms that which is in itself ineffable.
> Art has a unique capacity to take
> one or other facet of the message and
> translate it into colors, shapes, and
> sounds which nourish the intuition
> of those who look or listen. It does so
> without emptying the message itself of
> its transcendent value and its aura of
> mystery . . . In Christ, God has recon-
> ciled the world to himself. All believers
> are called to bear witness to this; but
> it is up to you, men and women who
> have given your lives to art, to declare
> with all the wealth of your ingenuity*

that in Christ the world is redeemed:
the human person is redeemed, the
human body is redeemed. This is your
task. Humanity in every age, and even
today, looks to works of art to shed
light upon its path and destiny. Artists
of the world, may your many different
paths all lead to that infinite Ocean
of beauty where wonder becomes awe,
exhilaration, unspeakable joy.[6]

Prayer as art is a mystery we experience. Symbols, sounds, colors, lines, words, and shapes become an avenue for the groans and longings of our hearts, artistically expressed. In an act of creativity we exercise our nature as beings made in the image and likeness of a Creator. Julia Cameron, author of *The Artist's Way,* a course on recovering our creativity, believes that opening ourselves to our own creativity opens us to God. Our yearning to create emanates from a divine source, and as we move toward it, we move closer to God and closer to being who God created us to be. Art as prayer allows the imagination to be a gift of God and creativity a channel for God's life to flow in our lives and through our lives to nourish the prayers of others.

---

6   *The Pope Speaks, Volume 44* (The Sunday Visitor, Incorporated, 1999), 310.

5

PRAYER
IN NATURE

The best remedy for those who are
afraid, lonely, or unhappy is to go
outside somewhere they can be quite
alone with the heavens, nature, and
God. Because only then does one
feel that all is as it should be and
that God wishes to see people happy,
amidst the simple beauty of nature.
As long as this exists . . . there will
always be comfort for every sorrow,
whatever the circumstances may
be . . . nature brings solace in all
troubles.

—From *The Diary of a Young Girl*
by Anne Frank[1]

---

1   Anne Frank, H.J.J. Hardy, David Barnouw, Gerrold van der Stroom
    (Rijksinstituut voor Oorlogsdocumentatie, Netherlands. Gerechtelijk
    Laboratorium, 1989), 520.

MY BEST CHILDHOOD memories are wrapped in the embrace of the natural world. Nature was where I went to talk to God. It was where I could speak to God without censoring my thoughts or editing my feelings. I felt at peace and uplifted by nature's beauty. I stopped to listen to the sound of a brook in the woods like monks chanting praise, and stood with my eyes closed in prayer without words, taking in that refreshing sound and pretending it washed through me, creating in me a clean heart. I felt the gratitude flow out of me toward God. The meadows and trees, lakes and streams, woods and fresh air all felt like God's presence inviting me closer. A field of wildflowers come upon unexpectedly, the sound of the wind rustling leaves, the taste of a warm ripe raspberry picked off the bush, the smell of a spring morning, the terror of a storm. In nature God is immense and close, fearsome and beautiful, and I found a home for prayer.

My parents bought a dairy farm when I was five years old and moved from a neighborhood in St. Paul, Minnesota, where we had played on sidewalks and filled plastic pools of water in tiny adjoining backyards. On the farm when my brothers and sisters and I were not in school, doing chores, or at church, we were playing outside. In the summer we played house in the old milk shed, scaled the walls of the hay barn, rolled down the piles of corn in the corncrib, captured toads and salamanders, snakes and butterflies in glass jars and pails. At night we walked up the road to play softball with kids in the neighborhood. When it got dark, we played red light/green light with flashlights and caught lightning bugs.

The ominous sky during a tornado warning, first blue, then black, then the thunder and lightning and sometimes hail big as golf balls, followed the stillness that came before the grayish yellow swirling winds could move us indoors and down the cellar stairs to the southwest corner of the basement.

The cold winter months were endless in hindsight, but not as a child. Sledding, ice skating on backyard ponds and flooded frozen rinks, building igloos and snow forts kept us outside all day with little notice of temperatures below freezing. I loved the days when a blizzard canceled school. We went out to the billowy snow piles and dug tunnels big enough to crawl through. Inside them, the snow turned a shade of aqua blue like the ice packs in a summer cooler. I walked to the field behind my house and lay on my back to look up at the stars and sing:

Not here for high and holy things we
* render thanks to thee,*
but for the common things of earth,
the purple pageantry of dawning and
* of dying days,*
the splendor of the sea.
The royal robes of autumn moors, the
* golden gates of spring,*
the velvet of soft summer nights
the silver glistering of all the million,
* million stars,*
the silent song they sing.

—Geoffrey Studdert-Kennedy,
in *Hymnal 1982* (p. 9)

My best friend from junior high school loved the natural world, but always knew what to do when that world turned frightening. She was the one with the spare ski tip when my ski cracked and broke after a fall; she wrapped me in blankets when I developed hypothermia on an eighth grade canoe trip. Now a National Park Ranger in Alaska, during the five-month summer season, Mary encounters God in the natural world: in the rhythm, power, order, color, and beauty; from the boundary waters on a trek to the vast ocean on a sea kayak. On the smallest scale and the most immense, she is aware of God alone and silent in nature. She writes: "As a child I wanted to know if God exists. How does a person know *for sure,* I used to wonder. I remember staring for hours at the starry sky up in northern Minnesota, seeing the

Milky Way and feeling the immensity, and coming face to face with the question of my place in the universe. Who am I in all this?" Experiencing the power and beauty of nature is where Mary's prayer comes alive. It assures her of God's existence and her desire to live in harmony with nature.

I asked Mary how she prays in nature. It begins in feelings of awe and appreciation and then a sense of "bliss erupts and sometimes bubbles up into song! I feel reverence, respect, and humility in the perspective nature gives to me: that God is God and I am not. It is like hitting the reset button and recalibrating my life."

Prayer in nature offers peace, calm, a sense of place and belonging. Mary is grounded and restored by nature. "I love wilderness, because it is the creation unedited. You get to read the manuscript. I appreciate farmers, fishermen, and gardeners, stewards of the earth who appreciate and care for her. I am grateful to them and furious with the multitude of people who disregard, harm, consume, and disrespect our earth."

Many of us experience God in nature. We recall times we have stood before mountains, the ocean, the stars of night, or a simple breeze and felt in nature's beauty and power a deep, overwhelming appreciation for life and closeness to the Creator.

On a sunny, autumn morning, walking a country road lined with tall white pines and golden elm trees not far from the church I serve, I look up.

Against the blue sky I see splashes of red maple and yellow ash, bordered by deep green. A gentle breeze loosens the colorful leaves and pine needles and they drift sideways and down, their final drift through the air as they come to die, finding new purpose, fertilizing the earth. I have never passed another person walking on this road. Infrequently a car goes by; turning in to one of the driveways I pass. Prayer goes on here, whether I am here to notice it or not. Communion between what is finite and what is infinite; no one needs to be here for prayer to go on. The natural world gives glory to God simply by being what it is and doing what it was designed by its Creator to do. Though human beings are different, though we were made free with choices to make and efforts to exert to cooperate with God's will for us (we are not exactly like a tree), we do well to take clues from the natural world.

The air is sweet and clear, light travels across the trees and flowers as if dancing. Half of the hay is cut and what's yet to be cut blows back and forth in the breeze with grace. I savor the warm sun on my skin. I am alone for as far as I can see. Across the bright meadow I walk toward a threshold that opens into pinewoods. My heart opens in gratitude for the beauty, for my senses of sight and smell and sound. I look as far as I can see, and when I know I am alone I raise my arms to the sky and say: "Lift up your heart." I do not ask for things; my prayer is simply gratitude. For my legs that got me here, for the gift of faith that moves prayer from my head to

my heart, for the experience of this prayer: me with
God in nature.

All will come again into its strength:
the fields undivided, the waters undammed,
the trees towering and the walls built low.
And in the valleys, people as strong
and varied as the land.

And no churches where God
is imprisoned and lamented
like a trapped and wounded animal.
The houses welcoming all who knock
and a sense of boundless offering
in all relations, and in you and me.

No yearning for an afterlife, no looking
    beyond,
no belittling of death,
but only longing for what belongs to us
and serving earth, lest we remain unused.

—From *The Book of Pilgrimage*,
by Rainer Marie Rilke[2]

We have these moments, but we do not know
what to call them, how to think of them as prayer.
We dive into the ocean waves or the clear water of a
lake and are overcome with refreshment. We see a
crab apple or magnolia in full spring bloom. It is so
beautiful it seems to have fallen from heaven.

In the midst of an active life, we can dedicate the

---

2   *Rilke's Book of Hours*, 121. Used by permission.

time we spend in nature to prayer. The awe, appreciation, and adventure are part of our prayer. Affirm your love of nature, letting it grow, and be part of your experience of and relationship with God. Prayer in nature draws our finite life into infinite life.

In *New Seeds of Contemplation,* Thomas Merton writes of the way elements in nature exist and give glory to God.

> *A tree gives glory to God simply by being a tree . . . it is expressing an idea which is not distinct from the essence of God, and therefore a tree imitates God by being a tree. The more a tree is like itself, the more it is like God. If it tried to be like something else which it was never intended to be, it would be less like God and therefore it would give God less glory. It is not as simple for human beings as it is for trees; we are given freedom to be whatever we would like to be. We are free to work with God in the creation of our life, our identity and destiny or not. The more we can be like a tree, an expression in human form not distinct from God, but imitating God's essence, the more God is part of this world, and we are beams from the light of God. As we become ourselves, our energy and creativity given us by God is manifested in our work and activity.[3]*

---

3 Thomas Morton, *New Seeds of Contemplation* (New York: New Directions Publishing; 2007), chapter 5.

In order to host a summer school program at our inner-city church, we needed to turn our backyard into a playground. Through the sweat and resources of partner churches, we opened a playground with swings and slides, climbing structures, a basketball hoop and hopscotch platform not only for our church and summer school, but for the surrounding neighborhood. The playground became a place of welcome, of evangelism, a place to sit and watch children play, to rest under the shade of a tree, to jump and run on grass, to run through a sprinkler on a hot day, to collect stones and paint them. Children went off on a school bus to swim at the local beach, returning wet and refreshed to eat watermelon before going home, letting it run down their faces as we hosed ourselves off on the playground.

Prayer originates in God, not us. We do not pray in the same ways we set out to improve our physical well-being through exercise, our emotional health through psychotherapy, our technological knowledge through a computer training course. We initiate these measures to gain something, to increase our knowledge or improve our relationships. Prayer is different. God takes the initiative, first giving us life and continuing to give us breath. Prayer is our response to what God has already begun in us: God's initiative, providing us with a soul in a human body that is in relationship to the Divine and Infinite.

The geography of the earth charts the interior landscape of our spirit, the contours of a road's bends, the dappled light of the shade through a canopy of trees; it is prayer and it is often captured best when we need words (or we might explode) by poetry.

I live my life in widening circles
that reach out across the world.
I may not complete this last one
but I give myself to it.

I circle around God, around the
primordial tower.
I've been circling for thousands of years
And I still don't know: am I a falcon,
a storm, or a great song?

—From *The Book of Monastic Life*,
by Rainer Maria Rilke[4]

Jay, a recent college graduate, told me he went to church occasionally but never associated with any of his fellow college students who called themselves "religious." I asked Jay where he prayed and how he connected to God. "Nature does it for me. That is where I feel God, and know God exists. Nature is my church. Nature just gives and gives and gives and I didn't do one thing to get it. Just think about a tree. It grows from inside itself. I do nothing to keep it going, it is all from God. Humans didn't do nature, we didn't create it, and it is always giving us everything that is essential to us, like air, water, fire, earth. The beauty of it is amazing. I can never

---

4   *Rilke's Book of Hours*, 48. Used by permission.

be in nature without thinking about God and feeling grateful."

> *I find you there in all these things*
> *I care for like a brother.*
> *A seed, you nestle in the smallest of them,*
> *and in the huge ones spread yourself hugely.*
>
> *Such is the amazing play of the powers:*
> *they give themselves so willingly,*
> *swelling in the roots, thinning as the*
> *   trunks rise,*
> *and in the high leaves, resurrection.*
>
> —From *The Book of Monastic Life*,
>   by Rainer Maria Rilke[5]

There are many ways to pray in nature. Working as an environmental scientist or engineer, organizing and editing manuscripts to benefit the natural world we have been given, working for its preservation and future can be a way of praying.

---

5   *Rilke's Book of Hours*, 68. Used by permission.

6

PRAYER
IN ADVERSITY

HOW DO WE pray when life is difficult? Some of us draw close to God when we are angry, hurt, sorrowful, or in trouble. God is a source of comfort to us; One who understands our plight, and hears our cries for help. Others of us find that our anger and hurt drive us away from God.

My brother-in-law was our children's and their cousins' favorite uncle. Stephen was the pied piper they followed in a pack at family reunions. His care-free spirit was exhibited in his bright, off-the-wall clothes and ever-changing haircuts, including his famous "no hawk mohawk," which left a thin strip of hair traveling down the center of his otherwise bald head. He wrote "Most Available" rather than "Stephen" on his nametag and played one-on-one basketball like a pro, his sweat and breath smelling of beer. He was ready to play and party any time of day or night; ready with a broad smile, quick to rub your shoulders and give you a hug as he flew by, always on to the next adventure.

Stephen's struggle with addiction began after high school and grew worse in his twenties and thirties, as his life was slowly engulfed by drinking, drugs, and a nomadic lifestyle. Even then, nothing dampened his spirit for long; he enrolled in culinary school and became a chef. After a difficult and dangerous period of drug use, forced hospitalizations and treatment, he was diagnosed with bipolar disorder. Once he completed treatment and rehab, he neglected to take his medication, had no interest in referrals for therapy, and we watched his illness grow worse. Tragically, his life ended in suicide when he was forty years old, a wrenching loss for our family and his many friends.

My mother-in-law, Stephen's mom, is a devout Roman Catholic. In her grief and despair, she lost her appetite for food and life, but still got up and went to Mass and "adoration," her mid-week hour of silent prayer where she kept company in her parish chapel with the sacrament that sustained her. Suicide is a sin in her church.

I went to adoration with her one morning and after we had sat together in silence, we walked behind the church to visit Stephen's burial site. Sitting on a wooden bench in the morning sun, I asked her if she was angry with God. She looked at me as though my question came from outer space. It never crossed her mind to be angry with God. "Cathy, Christ has been with me and has been my best friend through this. Damn that Stephen, God knows how I loved that boy." God was not her judge. God was her companion: merciful and understanding.

There's a wideness in God's mercy,
* like the wideness of the sea;*
there's a kindness in his justice, which
* is more than liberty.*
There is no place where earth's sorrows
* are more felt than up in heaven;*
there is no place where earth's failings
* have such kindly judgment given.*

—Fredrick W. Faber,
in *Hymnal 1982* (p. 470)

Prayer walks with us through the valley of the shadow of death. "Even there your hand supports me, Your right hand holds me fast," Psalm 23 reminds us. Throughout the scriptures the message is clear: God stays close to us when we hurt. God is present in times of trouble whether we feel it or not. The scriptures remind us again and again that God is familiar with suffering, acquainted with grief, and offers us consolation, mercy, and aid. The help often arrives in disguise. Some people, like my mother-in-law, feel it and know it at the time they experience it: embraced, upheld by God in a myriad of ways: through people that care about them, through the strength they receive from the prayers and community around them.

A mother I know lost two sons, one to illness, the other to violence, ten years apart. She drew close to her community of faith and depended on their help and support. "My church was always there for me. I tend to be kind of private, not asking for help much, even from God. I tried to go it alone and be strong. When my second son died, I knew I couldn't do it by myself. I knew God was with me each and every step of the way. I kept a journal to keep me sane and when I read it, no question: God was there for me. I didn't always feel it, I had to believe without the feelings." Her pastor taught the congregation to pray out loud so that others could hear your prayers and pray with you. She could listen to others pray for her when she could not find the strength to pray for herself. He set up a prayer phone chain as a way for people to stay connected to each other through prayer in hard times.

"I was never angry at God. My boss gave me that book *When Bad Things Happen to Good People* and I read it a little, but I don't think like that. Bad things happen to everyone; being good or bad is not really the point, is it?" She told me she was never angry at God. She was angry at our violent culture, and angry at her son's illness. Not God. Every challenge and loss she went through brought her closer to God. "No one should feel sorry for me for the losses I have been through. I would rather we all understand that the bad stuff that happens to us is what gives us our strength, those experiences are what have caused me to grow close to God, and care more for other people."

Not everyone has the experience these two mothers share with us. For others, suffering and loss are times when we feel forgotten by God. Physical, mental, or emotional pain erects a wall between us and God. It's as if a steel door slams shut. No God of love would allow this to happen to me. We run as far away as we can. We cannot go to church; we cannot listen to what sounds like the false promises of a loving Creator who allows such a tragedy to happen to us or someone we love. Our pain builds a barrier of protection around us and we close ourselves off.

"When my father died, I was so angry at God I stopped going to church." She stood up from her pew in the white-walled school chapel, athletic and beautiful, a bright scarf against her black skin, her eyes intense with light and intelligence. "Why did God do that to me?" Her dad took her to church every Sunday. It was the only time all week that she sat next to him. They belonged together, just the two of them in the quiet beauty of worship. He often reached for her hand as they listened to the sermon. They sang the hymns together. Her anger at God had kept her from entering a church since the day of his funeral.

I meet with people who only darken the door of a church with a sense of obligation. They attend a service with family or friends when visiting for a holiday, or when there is a death in the family and we meet to plan a service in my office. I often hear the anger that has come between them and God. "I used to love church. But we've been trying to have a child for years. Our infertility feels like God's punishment. What did I do wrong to deserve this? All I ever wanted was to be a mother. I come to church and see all these little kids running around and happy families going up to communion together. It seems they all take having children for granted. I hate coming to church."

A friend lost her daughter several days after giving birth. Suddenly the heart of a person who prayed daily slammed shut. She tried to pray, but gave up, feeling phony. My friend lost faith in God's care for her; she didn't feel God's presence. Losing her baby isolated her from other people; no one seemed to understand the depth of her loss—not her husband, not her mother, not her closest friends. People would say: "Imagine how awful it would be to lose a child you raised," as if her loss was nothing. One morning after her son left for school and her husband for work, she went to her desk to write. She sat down and was gripped by anger. The emotion was so intense, she did not know what to do. Should she call someone? She thought of screaming or throwing dishes against the kitchen wall. I'll go running, she thought, and sat on the edge of the bed to lace up her sneakers. She had one shoe on when she turned and let her face fall into the pillow. Clenching her fists, she began hitting the pillow harder and harder: crying, then yelling, and then screaming. Her rage was so immense, it scared her. As she threw one fist after the other into the pillow, the pillow began to feel like something other than a pillow. She began to see in it the chest of Jesus, his sacred heart. She kept on pummeling her pillow and Jesus was taking it, even encouraging her rage. She felt the compassionate presence of God. The heart of

Jesus was with her in her loss; expressing her anger gave the spirit an opening to move into her experience. She pounded the pillow, blasting her angry fists onto the loving heart of God.

Rage can be prayer. Our anger is no less God's creation than calm is. Anger comes from God, just as peace does. Blame God, be mad at God, hold God responsible, do anything but block God from what hurts.

What do you do when you are angry with someone you care about? Often I push them away, avoid them, not returning an email or call. Or I find the courage to go and talk to them, as uncomfortable as it might be. It is the same with God; we stop going to church, stop praying, become self-sufficient, independent. Unable to conceive of the God we are running from being acquainted with grief and despair like ours, and wanting, by whatever means, to break through to us, we run away. Who needs a God like that! In Psalm 139 we read of the instinct to turn away from God: "Where can I hide from your presence, where can I flee from your spirit? If I take the wings of the morning and dwell in the uttermost parts of the sea, even there your hand leads me, your right hand holds me fast."

Anger is energy, powerful energy. If we ignore it, hoping it will go away, most often it doesn't. Anger has a purpose. Anger is on a mission and wants to accomplish something. Unexpressed anger clouds our sight and colors our experience. It goes underground and causes depression. Or it flares up at the wrong person at the wrong time and ends a friend-ship, costs us a marriage or a job.

Pray when you are angry. Pray when you are hurt. Pray when you are in trouble. The hardest part is to be where we are and begin there. We want to be somewhere else, somewhere that feels more peaceful and less messy. Praying with my anger is not soothing or peaceful. Rage wants to explode outward. Jesus overturned tables while yelling at people, telling them that the temple was not a mar-ketplace. Jesus walked into a street fight where a woman caught in adultery was being pummeled with rocks. He invited the first person free of sin to throw the next stone. Jesus was angry with his dis-ciples who often exasperated him.

Pray as you hit a pillow (not a person), talk to someone, vent while you run with someone you can talk to, hit tennis balls, baseballs, play squash, close the windows in your car and yell. Write when you are angry. Pray with your anger, even when you cannot figure out what to do with it. Even this can be a prayer: "I am angry, God, and I have no idea what to do, how to share it with you, or let you into this. I am angry that you let this happen to me, that you don't seem to care about me. God, where were you? How could you? Where are you?"

Praying when we are angry opens a door. It is an act of courage to pray with our anger. And it is the beginning of letting God heal and repair what is broken.

The Kingdom

It's a long way off but inside it
There are quite different things going on:
Festivals at which the poor man
Is king and the consumptive is
Healed; mirrors in which the blind look
At themselves and love looks at them
Back: and industry is for mending
The bent bones and the minds fractured
By life. It's a long way off, but to get
There takes no time and admission
Is free, if you will purge yourself
Of desire, and present yourself with
Your need only and the simple offering
Of your faith, green as a leaf.

—R. S. Thomas[1]

Being able to sense God's presence is a gift, yet sometimes we are not given that gift. Sometimes we are left without a sense of God's presence. We rely on the history of our faith, its stories, and its faithful people to give us conviction, beyond feeling, that we cannot muster for ourselves. We listen as those around us pray on our behalf. God accompanies us at a level deeper than feeling. I will never forget reading a sermon written by a father who lost his child. He said many things, but all I remember

---

1 *Collected Poems 1945–1990* (London: Phoenix Press, 1993), 233. Used by permission.

is this: "I have been to the bottom," he said, "and it is solid."

Anger is God's creation, designed to teach us, protect us, and deepen our friendship with God; particularly when adversity strikes. If abandonment by God is what you feel, let it be part of your prayer. Jesus did. When he felt abandoned by his friends, he asked them to stay awake with him. When Jesus most needed to feel God's presence, he did not. "My God, My God why have you forsaken me?" was his cry. In those pain-filled, honest questions, we are granted to see the presence of God.

Do the best you can. Start where you are. Try being kind to yourself. Let others help. Being prayed for and cared for by a community is an extraordinary gift when we cannot or do not know how to pray for ourselves.

7

FOSTERING PRAYER IN DAILY LIFE

PLANS I WAS trying to make were foiled by schedule conflicts. Tasks I was attempting to complete were interrupted by phone calls. I let an email lure me off in another direction. Stopping to pray would help me find a center in my day; it would reduce my frustration. But I didn't want to pray. I wanted my mind to stop jumping around like a monkey. My frustration increased my determination to get stuff done. I told myself to finish this one thing and then I would feel at peace and could stop to pray. I finished that one thing—and it led to the next thing. The problem I was having is this: I did not want to be where I was and consequently did not want to pray, because to pray is to be in the present moment. I didn't want to say: "God, I'm anxious, I'm worried. All these things need to be done. Why don't you ease up on what you ask of me? Help me. Be with me." Wherever we are, no matter our mood, our day, our circumstance: it is a place for prayer.

My first year of seminary was Bishop Krister Stendahl's last year as dean at Harvard Divinity School. I was in the final class ordained by Bishop

John Coburn (bishop of the Episcopal Diocese of Massachusetts) before his retirement. These two men were my teachers, mentors, and friends. They were scholars and theologians for whom prayer was the centerpiece of Christian faith.

I visit Brita, Krister's wife, and we talk about Sweden, and books, the news, and missing Krister. Once, when I visited her on Nantucket Island (visit Stockholm and you understand why Swedes love islands and water), we talked about prayer. Brita confessed to me that Krister prayed so beautifully, she let him pray for both of them. "I just slipped along his radiant pathways and mumbled my amens! But when I was on my own, it was a very different story." Krister could no longer put Brita's needs and gratitude into words to God, and she did not know how to begin. "It was a jungle of beginnings, stops, ideas, starting over, and often just: Oh, dear God, where am I?"

She discovered, as if for the first time, a prayer she'd been saying for years. "The prayer for me was The Lord's Prayer: short sentences, everything I need expressed in a few lines, heaven, earth, food, life, death, good and evil." Using the prayer as her own, she began to pray in a whole new way. "My eyes opened and I prayed watching kids at the playground, reading the daily newspaper, driving my car, going shopping. Prayers formulated themselves in my mind when a scene came before my eyes. I'd see good and evil in the news, terrible horrors, and ask God to keep me close. 'Lead us not into temptation' I prayed as I read the daily paper. Now, wherever I go, and whomever I meet, there is a spark within me. I watch the world, and without me doing anything, there is prayer. Prayer is a form of life."

> *Seven whole days, not one in seven,*
> * I will praise thee;*
> *in my heart, though not in*
> * heaven, I can raise thee.*
> *Small it is, in this poor sort to*
> * enroll thee;*
> *e'en eternity's too short to extol thee.*
>
> —George Herbert,
> in *Hymnal 1982* (#382)

As we exercise the muscle of prayer, it becomes stronger, more agile. The more I walk, the stronger my legs get; the more we pray the more it supports us. As we cultivate our ability to offer our life's work, our relationships, our anger, our art, our actions, and our bodies to God as instruments to be used, prayer is less a duty or obligation. Prayer becomes something we cherish and find ways to savor and foster as a form for life.

Many people have been hurt by experiences they have had in church. Life's losses may cause us to feel betrayed or rejected by God and the church. If this has happened to you, talk to a trusted guide, a priest, a friend, a pastor who can help bring your experience out of the darkness into the light. You are not alone. You may have stepped away for very good reasons. Perhaps it is time to come back.

I believe God wants to be a part of our life, to bring us companionship, affirmation, understanding, forgiveness, and joy. Pray. When you find yourself reacting negatively to church, let it enter your prayer, talk with God about what you have experienced. Accept where you are, listen to yourself, let your fears or what went wrong be the first thing you begin to pray about. Be open to prayer leading you to a life-affirming, challenging experience of the Spirit of God at work in your life.

Prayer always takes place in the present. Not unlike breathing. We can't take a breath in the past, not can we breath for the future; breathing exists for the present moment. As we practice prayer, we come more fully into the present moment.

> *The sixteenth-century Jesuit Jean-Pierre de Caussade wrote one book,* Abandonment to Divine Providence, *90 pages in length, published 100 years after his death. He offers an artistic metaphor for surrendering ourselves to the divine action in our lives. We are a "canvas waiting for the brush, or marble under the sculptor's hands." We attend to the duties of the present moment, not by a mysterious spiritual search to attain some height of surrender, but by simply being in the present moment*

and regarding it as a sacrament where
we meet God. Come, I say, come not
to study the map of the realms of the
spirit, but to possess it so that you can
walk freely about it and never be afraid
of getting lost. Come not to study the
record of God's grace, not to learn what
it has done down all the centuries and
is still doing but come be the trusting
subject of its operation.[1]

Fear of the future—not just the big future, but worrying right now about tonight and missing this afternoon, or stewing over what I said this morning or wishing I'd never said what I did last night— keeps us from the present moment where God waits to meet us. Prayer is an antidote to fear and anxiety. It opens us to the Infinite Source of all we will need not only for today, but for right now.

The devil despises the present moment. The Spirit of Darkness does all it can to draw us backward or lure us forward. The Adversary, the elemental power in the universe that is never for us, but always against us, seeks to draw us away from God. Learn the voice; notice how often you hear a voice seeking to undermine your efforts: *Pray in the car? Don't you have a better time for God than this? Pray in a boardroom? God doesn't listen in an*

---

1   Jean-Pierre de Caussade, *Abandonment to Divine Providence* (Colorado Springs: Image Books, 1993), 56.

office! Stop wasting God's time and yours. Get busy, do something worth your while. Walking is not real prayer, it's exercise. How could the Creator be in your creativity when your painting looks so bad and your poems never sell? The Adversary is not hard to figure out; it will use any means to try to keep you from God. *Oh, give it up, get busy, do something productive, you're no good at prayer* are some of the sly, wily power's favorite lines.

Julia Cameron calls it the Censor and, through her book *The Artist's Way,*[2] warns artists that it "resides in our left brain and keeps up a constant stream of subversive remarks often disguised as the truth . . . the Censor is out to get you, it is a cunning foe. Every time you get smarter, so does it. It loves to aim at your creative jugular." She advises us to think of our "Censor as a cartoon serpent, slithering around your creative Eden, hissing vile things to keep you off guard." Making it into a nasty, clever character begins to loosen its power.

We resist the adversarial voice by asking for protection from it, by laughing at it when we recognize it (oh you again, you're such a bore, go away). Expect the voice, don't be surprised by it, remind yourself that it shrinks and shrivels to nothing before the light and love of God. Pray for protection, and the power of God which has no match will come to your aid.

---

2   Julia Cameron, *The Artist's Way: A Spiritual Path to Higher Creativity* (New York: The Penguin Group, 1992), 11.

Nike got it right: "Just do it."

It is true of exercise and true of practicing an art like writing, painting, or dancing. Thinking about it, talking about doing it, buying new pens and a notebook or running shoes is still not doing it. Praying is something we just do, we try it, we try again, we go back to it every day. We get better, we grow more comfortable, we forget, sometimes for weeks or months or years. Just start over. Stay with it. It helps to enjoy the form of prayer you practice.

Enjoy God. Approach prayer as you would a new friend you want to get to know, a new book you can't wait to read. A friend told me she wanted to pray in the morning, but she loved sitting by herself with a cup of coffee to prepare for the day ahead. It never dawned on her to bring her morning coffee to prayer. Practice prayer in ways that are pleasurable. Pray in the myriad of ways this book has presented, while running, practicing yoga, at the art museum, at work, listening to music. Pray in thanksgiving in the woods or under a tree in a city park; pray while cooking or gliding across a lake in a kayak. All these gifts are from God. Enjoy God.

Prayer can be practiced at any time or place. And when possible it helps to have *a place* you go to that is a retreat; a chair by the window, a bench outside, a chapel in the hospital, a place in the park, a corner of your room or office. Make it an appealing place and, if possible, a place where you will not be disturbed. If the only time you find to pray is in the car or at the kitchen sink, claim them as places of prayer. Post something there—a beautiful photograph or a word of scripture—something you love to look at that will invite your prayer.

When it is possible, *choose a time* you will offer God your undivided attention. Make it a small amount of time you are able to commit to without strain. I know one person who wakes up and takes 10 minutes to pray before getting out of bed. Someone else talks with God in the shower where no one else will interrupt him. If you think 30 minutes is about the right amount of time for you, then begin with 15 minutes, and add 15 more when you find yourself meeting the goal of 15 minutes with ease and regularity.

Decide how to spend the time before it begins. Commit the time to silent meditation, or reading the scriptures and savoring it, writing in a journal, walking or being in conversation with God or Jesus about your upcoming day, or the day that has passed. Change the form you choose from one season of the year to another so you will look forward to trying something new. While this book is about the practice of unceasing prayer in daily life, silent prayer offers us the presence of God in a manner unlike any other form of prayer. *Centering Prayer* by Thomas Keating is a helpful guide to a practice of silence.

Invite negative voices that criticize you and diminish the importance of prayer *to leave.* If you hear "this is stupid" or "this is boring" or "what a waste of my time on a busy day," tell the voice to leave. It is not from God. It is trying to pull you away from God. Open the door and invite it out.

Choose a mantra, a line or phrase, as you get up from your prayer that will enable you to pray as you go about your day. Some suggestions are: "Thank you," "Help me," "Stay with me," "Guide me," "Give me strength," "Pray in me," "Thy will be done," "Into your hands."

Find a community for your practice of prayer. Look and you will find a church, synagogue, mosque, or meditation center to belong to. Be warned: faith communities are communities of human beings. You will be disappointed, encountering things that you do not like, but stay. The benefits of your membership will reveal themselves to you, and you will be a benefit to those you join. Practice not judging others.

Speak to God as you go about your day with honest, simple words. Ask for what you need. Practice gratitude as a life stance, independent of events that make you feel happy or sad. Do not assume God knows everything: talk to God. The Spirit within each of us connects us to the Spirit of God, that Spirit listens to us and guides us when we ask for help and direction. God has initiated the desire in you to pray; your prayer is a response to God's invitation.

Praying
It doesn't have to be
the blue iris, it could be
weeds in a vacant lot, or a few small stones; just
pay attention, then patch

a few words together and don't try
to make them elaborate, this isn't
a contest but the doorway
into thanks, and a silence in which
another voice may speak.

—Mary Oliver[3]

---

3 In *Thirst* (Boston: Beacon Press, 2006), 37.